Fatal Reunion

A criminal game of attraction

James Rosenberg

Allie H Publishing

THIS BOOK IS DEDICATED to the lifelong friends made during the summers spent in Su-Chip battles, playing prisoner's base, flipping baseball cards, sky high night at the park, archery and softball leagues. But mainly it's for the lifelong memories and life lessons that have made us all better people as adults.

Chapter 1

THE VERTICAL GLASS WINDOWS stretched the length of the wall parallel to the court, letting in faint trickles of light as afternoon surrendered to dusk. With no ventilation, the collective odor of the players lingered in the rafters. The squeak of basketball shoes sliding across the parquet floor echoed against the brick walls.

Ten players, each drenched in sweat, squatted into defensive crouches and set picks like the pros they mimicked on TV. There were no spectators and no chance that their games would ever be televised.

Sam Jordan—no relation to Michael—was the youngest and tallest on the court. Aside from his buddy Gregg, everyone else was at least a decade older and thirty pounds heavier.

This was Sam's domain. He secured access to the facility, which hosted dodgeball for kids during the day and dance practice after school hours. He also took on the responsibility of sending out texts to rally players, which conveniently gave him the authority to decide who played on which team.

Dressed in red shorts emblazoned with the white "W" of his undergraduate alma mater, Wisconsin, and with his arms encased in black compression sleeves, Sam positioned himself near the foul line and demanded the ball. While no one considered him a star baller, he was the best of the group assembled that evening. Despite scoring half his team's points, they trailed by one basket.

"Find me. Find me, George!" Sam yelled, darting beyond the three-point line as his teammate puttered with the ball. Instead of passing, the man with the gold terrycloth headband put his head down and drove toward the hoop. He didn't get there as one of the quicker players on the opposing team stripped the ball away before he could shoot.

With two swift passes, the other team sank an easy layup to clinch the win.

Sam stood still as the final play unfolded, watching the ball swish through the net, his arms crossed. "Stupid shit," he muttered as the players drifted off the court. He shuffled to the bench, shaking his head, and sidled up to Big George. "Pass it next time," he said, drawing out the word "pass" to emphasize his irritation.

"Whatever," George replied, stuffing his gear into his bag without turning to face Sam, which only stoked Sam's ire.

"Dude," Sam said, grabbing George's shoulder and giving it a slight pull. "Don't 'whatever' me."

George shrugged off Sam's hand. "It's just a pickup game. Other people want to shoot too."

"You couldn't even get a shot off," Sam snapped, shoving the larger man from behind. George stumbled forward, crashing into the first row of wooden bleachers.

Despite the embarrassment, George took a moment to collect himself. He stood, walked deliberately toward Sam, and stared him down with a sneer. "What the hell is your problem?"

Sam smirked as the bigger man loomed over him. "Get out of my face. Go back to Walmart and stock some batteries."

George lunged, hands reaching for Sam's face, but Gregg jumped between them, wrapping his arms around Sam and pulling him away to the far side of the gym.

"Buddy," Gregg said as Sam glared across the court. "What are you doing? This isn't worth it."

Sam jabbed a finger in George's direction. "That fat turd sucks at basketball."

"True," Gregg said, shrugging. "But is it worth fighting over?"

"I can't stand people who can't play," Sam grumbled.

Gregg studied his friend, then shook his head. "This isn't about basketball, is it?" He poked Sam's chest.

Sam grimaced. "I'm messed up," he admitted. "Jenny leaving. Barely seeing my kid. Working crazy hours." He shrugged again.

"I get it," Gregg said. "Still not worth losing your mind over a pickup game."

Sam exhaled and managed a sheepish smile. "You're right. But seriously, that guy's terrible." He draped an arm over Gregg's shoulders. "Let's grab a beer. We can trash talk everyone else instead."

The two friends gathered their gear and headed for the exit. On the way out, Sam caught George's eye. "Same time next week, big guy."

George nodded and then shook his head as Sam left, stuffing the last of his gear into his bag.

Chapter 2

T HE SMALL, DANK TOWNHOUSE didn't offer much promise. A petite woman stood in the doorway, her gaze sweeping over the barren interior. The only furnishings were a bean bag chair tossed in the middle of the living room and a tiny flat-screen perched precariously on a milk crate in the corner.

She stepped into the kitchen, placed a hand on the laminate countertop, then immediately wiped it on her jeans.

Sam trailed behind her, his eyes fixed on the floor. "Well," he mumbled, "this is where I'm staying. For now."

She turned to him, forcing a smile. "It's nice," she said, her tone lifting into an almost-question. "I'm sorry you couldn't find anything better. I didn't give you much time."

Sam winced. He'd secured the place just a week earlier after Jenny asked him to leave. Her visit now gave him a flicker of hope that their separation might still be temporary.

Standing next to Jenny felt awkward, the distance between them almost tangible.

Memories of their wedding day surged unbridled into his mind. She had been radiant in her flowing gown, her beauty so striking it had made his hands tremble as he slipped the ring onto her finger. Friends teased him about "punching above his weight class," and he'd laughed along, knowing they were right. The day had been perfect, even if he'd drunk too much at the reception and vomited on the hotel bed. Back then, the entire world awaited them.

Eight years ago, they brimmed with potential. Fresh out of law school, they'd landed coveted jobs at respected firms. Their weekends were filled with friends, and they could always had their families to turn to for advice when needed.

For a while, everything followed the plan. Jenny climbed the ladder quickly, making partner within four years. Her star kept rising, unimpeded by any obstacles.

Sam's career, by contrast, meandered. He left his first firm in less than two years, though he managed to transition to another job without the indignity of being fired. But after nearly three years at the second firm, issues with time management led to a sudden exit. His third job took months to find and also ended poorly after just 18 months.

When he told Jenny it was because the firm was losing clients, she believed him. She never voiced doubts about his potential, always steadfast in her support.

Now, at his fourth firm, Sam knew partnership was an illusion—not that it mattered much at this particular firm. The indignation of taking home so much less than Jenny gnawed at him, chipping away at his self-esteem. Deep down, though he never admitted it, he resented how effortless success was for her.

Jenny broke the silence. "I just wanted to see how you were doing," she said with a smile that Sam couldn't help but read as condescending.

"So good," he replied, throwing his hands up. "Why wouldn't I be? Look at this place. It's the dream, right? At this rate, I'll be living in a trailer by the river next year."

He turned back toward her, attempting a confident smirk that landed closer to pathetic. "This sucks," he said bluntly. "Explain to me again why we're doing this."

Jenny flushed. "We've talked about it, and we'll talk more. Just not now." She took a step closer. "I came over to discuss three things." She paused, waiting for a response, but Sam only rolled his eyes. "First, Nathan misses you. It's been a few days, and he's confused."

"Of course he's confused!" Sam snapped. "One day he wakes up, and I'm gone. Wouldn't you be confused if that happened to you? I want to see him. I miss him. Can we all have dinner together?"

Jenny shook her head. "I think that might be too much for him right now. Why don't you pick him up tomorrow after work? My mom's in town babysitting, so you can take him out."

"Oh, I'm sure your mom will be thrilled to see me," he muttered. "What's the second thing?"

Jenny bit her lip. "This one might feel rougher, but it's not." She hesitated, but when he didn't respond, she pressed on. "Tomorrow, I'm having dinner with Bill Harkins. Remember him from law school?"

Sam frowned. "Yeah, I remember. Big guy, wavy hair, bit of a blowhard. Women liked him."

Jenny nodded. "He might refer a client to me."

Sam's stomach churned. "So that's why you want me to take Nathan. Convenient." His voice rose. "If it's just business, why are you telling me?"

Jenny sighed. "Because people might see us, and I didn't want you hearing about it secondhand. It's nothing. Just casual."

Sam struggled for a response. "Thanks for thinking of me," he finally muttered. "What's the third thing?"

Jenny stepped closer, placing a hand on his arm. "This might be the hardest," she said, pulling a manila folder from her bag. "These are divorce papers." She held them out to him.

"What? This was supposed to be temporary! You said you needed space to figure things out." He snatched the folder from her.

"I still don't know what I want," Jenny said gently. "But if we can't figure this out, I want us to be prepared for a clean separation. We don't have to do anything right now."

Sam didn't move.

"We'll talk more," she said, backing toward the door. She slid out without either of them saying another word.

The townhouse was silent, save for the low hum of the flat-screen. Sam stared at the folder in his hand, his mind racing back to law school. They'd been the cool kids then—the future stars. Everyone envied them. People were jealous. Jenny's future still shone bright. His had spiraled into a wreck.

With a bitter laugh, he threw the folder into the trash.

Chapter 3

S AM'S LATEST OFFICE WAS in the heart of downtown, housed in a small brick building with worn carpet in the lobby and a rickety elevator. The firm's claim to distinction lay in its unconventional setup: the entrance to their practice was on the fourth floor, with an interior staircase leading to the lawyers' offices on the fifth. The partners believed this added an air of sophistication. In reality, it probably just confused clients who inevitably arrived on the wrong floor.

Sunlight streamed through the window as Sam entered, casting prismatic colors on his desk. He paused to admire the effect. A pile of work overflowed his blotter—a sight that usually sharpened his focus. Today, he planned to dive in without delay.

After graduating from Pitt, Sam had landed a position with Hurley and Hill, a medium-sized firm renowned for its stellar reputation. Their offices occupied a prestigious class-one building with a view of the courthouse across the street. Proud of his achievements, Sam framed his college and law degrees alongside his admissions to the Pennsylvania Supreme Court and federal court. Matted with the finest of cotton fibers, he and Jenny spent a weekend hanging the diplomas in his small associate office. Together, they made the walls proclaim, "Here's a talented lawyer."

For a while, it worked. Sam billed ridiculous hours like everyone else, spending ungodly amounts of time researching obscure points of law that ended up as footnotes in massive briefs for the firm's well-heeled clients. But the paltry bonus he received after his first year—even after billing twenty-two hundred hours—was disheartening. Other associates were billing hundreds of hours more, setting a Sisyphean standard. Every morning, Sam would arrive at the office knowing eight hours of work wouldn't bring him any closer to catching up. Saturdays and Sundays became his catch-up days, spent staring at a computer screen, squeezing out more billable hours.

The relentless grind began taking a toll. Sleepless nights became routine as stress drove Sam to pace the apartment in the early hours. Jenny, on the other hand, managed her own demanding job with ease. She wanted weekends to be their time—to connect, have fun, and escape from work. But Sam's work had no off-switch.

By his second- and third-year reviews, cracks in Sam's performance were impossible to ignore. The partners labeled his research "substandard" and his attitude "confrontational." No one explicitly told him to leave, but Sam knew he had no future at Hurley and Hill. Late nights on the computer searching for jobs while Jenny slept became his new normal. After weeks of looking, he accepted a position at a slightly less prestigious firm. When he told Jenny about the change, she burst into tears. "I didn't even know you were thinking about leaving," she said.

But the new firm didn't offer the fresh start Sam hoped for. The cycle repeated, each move dragging him further down the professional ladder. Now, at his fourth firm, his resume had grown—but it was unimpressive.

Sam slammed his computer bag onto his desk at Morton and Gerber, a tiny firm with just three lawyers: the two named partners and him. The partners were relics from another era. Their suits were outdated, and the offices reeked of cigar smoke despite the building's strict no-smoking policy. At least Sam's office was down a separate hallway, offering a modicum of privacy.

He sank into his chair, ignoring the tears in the leather armrests. Plugging his computer into the docking station, the screen flickered to life. Unlike his work at larger firms, which focused on niche legal issues for corporate giants, Morton and Gerber handled a variety of smaller, less sophisticated matters. One day he'd draft articles of incorporation, the next he'd advise an elderly couple on their estate plans, and then he'd argue a motion to compel in a personal injury case. The variety was refreshing, even if the prestige was lacking.

At Morton and Gerber, Sam managed his cases independently—developing strategies, writing pleadings, and making critical decisions. He hoped these experiences were shaping him into a well-rounded attorney. The partners were gruff but generally fair. Still, Sam's skepticism about the firm lingered, especially on days when he dwelled on its lack of reputation. Jenny often reminded him that the smaller firm's pace and diversity of practice had advantages over handling only large corporate matters, but her words never convinced him.

Papers were strewn across his desk, begging for attention. Sam glanced at the piles, unsure where to start. He decided coffee might help and stood to head to the small kitchen across the hall.

Before he could leave, Gary Gerber waltzed in, a folder clutched to his chest. His gray and green sports coat strained at the seams, and a button nearly popped as he plopped into the worn leather chair across from Sam's desk.

Sam hesitated, disheartened that his coffee break would have to wait. "What's up, Gary?" He wanted to call him "Gerbs," the nickname everyone used behind his back, but he couldn't muster the nerve.

"We need to talk," Gerber said, avoiding Sam's gaze.

"About what?" Sam waved his hand, trying to catch his attention.

Gerber stood and began pacing, picking up a photo from Sam's bookshelf. "Nice family you've got. How old's your boy now?"

"Just turned four. Amazing little dude," Sam replied, guarded. He hadn't told anyone at work about his new living situation.

"Kids are great. Expensive, though. Keep having them." Gerber brushed imaginary lint off his pants. "Anyway, Sam, you've been here almost a year, and you're doing good work. Clients like you. You don't mind getting your hands dirty."

"Thanks," Sam said, unsure where this was going.

Gerber waved his hand dismissively. "This isn't about you. It's the firm. Revenue isn't where it used to be. Nothing's changing today, but if we—and I mean all of us—don't bring in more work, we're going to have a much harder conversation."

Sam's stomach dropped. His heart raced, and he struggled to breathe. It was the same gut-wrenching feeling he'd had every other time he'd lost a job. "I'm doing what I'm supposed to, aren't I? I'm here late. Like you said, clients aren't complaining."

Gerber nodded, already moving toward the door. "Sometimes bad things happen to good people," he said, disappearing into the hallway.

Sam slumped forward, resting his head on the desk blotter. He tapped his forehead against the surface—once, then twice, then again. It didn't make him feel any better. All he could think about was what blow life would deliver next.

Chapter 4

THE HOUR WAS EARLY, and darkness still cloaked the neighborhood as Sam entered Primo Coffee Shop. He nodded at the server behind the counter, who waved back. In the back corner, Gregg sat nursing a latte, his eyes fixed on his phone.

"Hey," Sam said, dropping his computer bag onto the table. "Let me grab my coffee, and I'll be back in a minute."

Gregg grunted but didn't look up, his dark green eyes glued to the screen.

Sam and Gregg had been friends since childhood, working as camp counselors during college and later landing in the same section in law school where they discovered they made a good team—Gregg excelled at Constitutional Law and Criminal Procedure, while Sam's knack for Torts helped demystify concepts like battery and defamation. They also shared a love for partying and took charge of organizing the class's weekly happy hours.

During their first year, Gregg and Jenny became friends, commuting together since they lived nearby. Initially, Sam had no romantic interest in Jenny; she was more of a third wheel to his and Gregg's budding "bro-mance." But in their final term, after one too many drinks on a Friday night, Sam and Jenny hooked up. Unlike most casual flings, theirs stuck. They began hanging out nearly every night, and when they married a year later, Gregg was the obvious choice for best man.

Post-graduation, all three found jobs in the city. Despite the demanding schedules of young attorneys, Sam and Gregg established a weekly ritual: coffee at dawn each Thursday. Gregg cherished the routine and always arrived early to secure a table by the window.

Since the rocky unraveling of Sam's marriage, Gregg had been careful not to take sides. If forced to choose, though, he'd back Sam. Their lifelong friendship outweighed his connection with Jenny, who seemed more self-sufficient anyway. Gregg focused on maintaining his friendship with Sam, keeping their shared activities—hoops, movies, beers—uninterrupted.

Jenny and Sam's separation was still fresh, and Gregg wasn't sure of the boundaries yet. He wanted to stay in touch with Jenny but assumed she'd respect his loyalty to Sam.

Sam returned with his coffee and opened his laptop. Their Thursday mornings usually involved an hour of emails, calls, and brief chats about their weeks, often seeking each other's input on tricky cases.

Sam typed furiously on his keyboard, while Gregg tapped at his phone. The steady hum of the coffee shop was punctuated by bursts of noise as college students entered, chatting loudly. Finally, Gregg glanced up.

"Hey, can I ask you a favor?"

Sam kept typing. "Sure, what's up?"

Gregg hesitated. "It's a little embarrassing."

Sam looked up, smirking. "Sexual difficulties?"

"No, nothing like that."

"Too bad. What is it?"

Gregg rolled his eyes. "I'm being sued."

Sam's fingers froze. "No way. For what?"

"Remember the woman from the gym I told you about months ago?"

"The one who complained about you and then disappeared?"

"That's her. She's claiming I harassed her. Now she's suing me."

"So it is about sex," Sam quipped.

"We never even dated," Gregg said, exasperated. "We talked a few times—barely that. Now she's accusing me of stalking her. She's claiming emotional distress and wants money."

Sam chuckled. "Has she filed a complaint?"

Gregg reached into his bag, pulling out a stapled document. He slid it across the table.

Sam skimmed the papers. "Is any of this true?"

"Of course not. The woman's nuts."

"Aren't they all?" Sam muttered, flipping to the last page. "Looks like you've got a hearing in a month."

"Yeah, I need an attorney. Know any good ones?"

Sam bit his lip. "Why not handle it yourself? You're a lawyer, or did you forget?"

"I know, but this is civil, not criminal. She doesn't want me in jail; she just wants money. And remember what Professor Lovitz always said?"

"A lawyer who represents himself has a fool for a client," they said in unison,

Both laughed. Gregg leaned back. "Exactly. I was hoping you'd help me out. There's nobody I trust more. I'll pay you."

"Won't take a dime," Sam said. "Even though you're a big-shot defense attorney now, making bank, this one's on me."

"Hey, I spent years at the DA's office making peanuts. I only just started earning real money. But thanks. I know you'll make her look ridiculous. You're the best."

Sam flushed. "Don't count on it. Just remember—you get what you pay for."

Chapter 5

THE DISCOUNT STORE HAD delivered the couch earlier in the week, along with a few other pieces of furniture. The solo bedroom now featured a bed with an inexpensive, square wooden frame. Dark gray sheets and a navy-blue comforter covered it, completing the minimalist setup.

On the kitchen counter, a knife block with plastic-handled knives sat alone. From a distance, it gave the illusion of being a high-quality set, but Sam knew it wasn't nearly as expensive as the one he and Jenny had received as a wedding gift. The realization depressed him. Checking out at Target with cheap towels, a soap dispenser, and a toilet brush had felt like rock bottom. The items screamed "low-rent" compared to everything Jenny had bought for their home. He even considered buying an AC/DC poster to complete the freshman-dorm vibe his place was giving off.

He slumped onto the couch, turned on the flat-screen, and opened Borderlands IV on his Nintendo. Playing video games at night wasn't how he had imagined spending his free time, but most of his friends were married, many were starting families, and none seemed to have time for someone newly single.

The game whirred to life as Sam propped a pillow behind his head, ready to immerse himself in the first-person shooter experience. During this new "alone time," he'd honed his arsenal of weapons and mastered various strategies to outwit opponents. He even passed along his wisdom to teammates online. Unfortunately, this growing skill set didn't translate well to his legal resume. He often wondered whether the guys he was playing with were acne-riddled teenagers or thirty-something men still living in their parents' basements.

During his third game—proudly undefeated for the evening—he noticed a notification on his phone. A message from Gina Marcon. The name sparked a flicker of recognition, though he couldn't place it immediately. After a pause, it clicked: Could this be someone from his distant past? Intrigued, he opened the message.

> "Is this the Sam Jordan I knew years ago?"

His pulse quickened as he replied:

> Possibly. Is this Gina Szeka from old Camp Hershey?

He waited. The reply didn't come right away, and his clammy hands gripped his phone. His team was getting destroyed in the game without its leader, but he no longer cared.

After what felt like an eternity, the familiar dots began blinking, signaling her response. When the notification pinged, Sam let out a relieved sigh and tapped the screen.

> This IS Gina Szeka. Wow, nobody's called me that in ages! I've been married for so long now. Those summers feel like a lifetime ago, but they're still some of my favorite memories. How are you doing?

Sam responded without hesitation. Unsure whether punctuation was "cool" in text messages, he remembered Jenny once teasing him about teens avoiding periods. Gina had used proper punctuation, so he decided to follow suit.

> I'm good! Married, one kid—he's four and awesome. Working as a lawyer (I am, not him). I really like my job. What about you? What's new?

He felt almost giddy. Gina Szeka. The queen of camp. Sweet, alluring, just out of reach. His stomach churned as long-suppressed memories surged back into his consciousness.

Before working at Camp Hershey, Sam's summers had been ordinary: playing with friends in grade school and lifeguarding at the community pool in high school. Family trips consisted of Sam and his two brothers crammed in the backseat or, in later years, sneaking beers with friends in the woods. It was fun but forgettable.

Two summers at camp changed everything. Rustic cabins, minimal adult supervision, and shared adventures redefined his views on relationships, fun, and life's priorities. "You can't understand unless you've been there," he would later explain to his family.

He arrived at camp in mid-June after his freshman year of college, seeking a break from the mundane. Persuaded by his friend Gregg—who raved about "no supervision," "uninhibited women," and "spectacular tans"—Sam signed up last-minute as a lake counselor. His mornings were soon filled with sailing lessons and swimming drills. Despite minimal experience with kids, he enjoyed their boundless enthusiasm. Sure, a few whined about cold water or venturing too far, but most loved motorboat rides or getting dunked during free swim.

Camp was a sensory overload. The lake's briny scent mingled with freshly cut grass from the ball fields. Even the stables' musky odor became part of the nostalgic tapestry. Years later, the scent of horses or freshly mowed lawns would instantly transport his mind back to the camp.

Three days before campers arrived, the administration hosted a mixer in the field house—a casual event with pizza and soda, designed to foster camaraderie. Music played, a few people danced, and everyone was eager to make a strong first impression.

Sam stuck close to Gregg and Mark, a tall, athletic sports counselor who didn't talk much. Just as the silence began to verge on awkward, two women approached.

The taller one extended her hand. "Hi, I'm Carrie Kellerman," she said, beaming. "And this is Gina. We just met."

Gina blushed, her jet-black hair falling over dark emerald eyes that sparkled when she smiled. The guys stammered out introductions, barely managing to ask about colleges and camp assignments.

Gina's hand brushed Sam's arm as she turned to him. "Want to grab a slice of pizza?" she asked. Her jasmine perfume lingered as they walked to the food table.

"I'm so glad to meet so many interesting people already," she said with a soft Southern lilt. Sam nodded, hoping his excitement wasn't obvious.

Before he could respond, she waved at another group. "Hey! I met them earlier—I want to ask them something." Touching his shoulder, she added, "So glad we met. We'll have plenty of time to get to know everyone."

Sam stood frozen, watching her walk away. He caught a faint wink—or maybe he imagined it—as she joined the other group. He blushed, hoping no one noticed his sudden surge of anticipation.

Chapter 6

S AM ARRIVED AT WORK prepared to dig into a couple of legal writing projects. One was a motion to compel in a breach of contract claim where the defendant refused to turn over what he believed were relevant documents. The other, a brief in support of his motion for summary judgment, requesting the court to dismiss the plaintiff's punitive damage claim in a tort action because there was no evidence to bolster such a small matter.

The summary judgment issue had been the focus of his attention for a few days, and he planned to bang out the other in an hour or two, so he thought he would complete the bulk of his to-do list by lunch and then focus on smaller matters in the afternoon. Always start with the bigger projects. Leave the little stuff for later. This was his customary plan of attack, a sound strategy, though it hadn't prevented him from losing all of his prior jobs.

The firm had one assistant for the three lawyers who also had responsibility for managing the office and helping with undefined paralegal work. Sam didn't receive much assistance and was responsible for drafting the bulk of the pleadings he filed with the court. Like most younger attorneys, he was proficient at formatting his documents and, unlike his bosses, didn't require help with typing, or with filing on the court's online platform.

He pulled LEXIS up on his computer to double-check his case citations and had the first brief opened on his second screen to make any necessary revisions. His flexed fingers hovered over the keyboard. With one more section to write, a solid hour's effort should be sufficient to complete the task and stop his client calling every two hours to check on its progress.

As his hands settled on the keys, his phone buzzed. Realizing he hadn't silenced the notifications, he grabbed it to turn them off, so he would focus. A wry smile crossed his face when another text from Gina appeared.

The temptation was too intense, so he opened it.

> Sam,
> hey. Just wanted to say hi.

He knew he should ignore it, at least for a while. Without thinking, he began to type:

> I'm here. Trying to write a
> brief.

Her reply came right away.

> I don't
> want to bother you. We can chat another
> time.

Sam's eyes didn't deviate from his phone. He wrote back:

> Not a problem. Would love
> to chat with an old friend.

> Good. I don't want to take up too much of
> your time, but I couldn't believe it's been
> fifteen years, and then, boom, we're talking
> again.

> I know. I want to hear more about your life.

He shouldn't be communicating with her, not now, but couldn't muster the strength to stop.

The blinking dots continued for a while, and then her response appeared:

> Let's see, since camp, I got a nursing degree.
> I work in the neo-natal unit of our hospi-
> tal. I'm living about two hours outside Pitts-
> burgh, so based on what I've seen online, we
> don't live that far apart.

He liked that she had been checking him out, but hoped she hadn't gotten the full update on his life.

> That sounds awesome. Like you're doing the good work. I try to think of the big picture with my work also.

He pushed the papers to the side and kicked his feet up on his desk. His leather chair swayed backwards with his weight. The dots again began to blink, and Sam's heart raced a bit quicker.

> So, you're a lawyer. Tell me about some of your big cases.

Sam deflected the question, and they went back-and-forth giving a few details of their lives until Sam asked:

> How's married life—any kids?

> My married life is just like everyone else's. I got an amazing husband. He has a great business and he's trying to build it up. Still don't have any babies, we've been putting it off, but we're ready. We just have fun. You know how it is.

He groused. Sure, love being married. Especially when your wife kicks you out and you don't see your kid much. A wave of annoyance swept through him. Why did everyone else's lives look so much better than his? He didn't deserve to be living in his tiny townhouse, forced to start over again.

> I understand what you're saying. I've been married for a while, but we're still having fun all the time. Always laughing and going places.

> Even with a kid?

> Sure. He's awesome. Turned four a few months ago. He takes a lot of energy, but we try to find time to hang out, just the two of us when we can. It works.

He smirked to himself.

> Wow, you seem to have your life so together. I can't wait to hear more. I got to go, but can we chat some more?

He nodded, though no one could see him. His fingers moved faster across his keyboard.

Of course. Can't wait. Whenever you have some time.

Once he realized their conversation was over, Sam was wasted, like after going to a huge party, having a great time and then coming home exhausted from putting out all of that energy. He looked over at the brief, in the same position as when they first started this chat and then realized he had spent almost two hours looking at his phone, waiting for her next communication to appear.

He grabbed the papers and placed them front and center to focus on finishing. So what if he had invested all this time catching up with a fantasy from his past? He'll work a little later this evening and catch up. It's no worse spending that time in the office alone chasing a memory, than wasting bad guys with an unknown bunch of sixteen-year-olds playing a video game.

The campers had arrived days earlier and were now settling comfortably into their new environment. Sure, there were a few bouts of homesickness, but for the most part, they had adapted to the rhythms of camp life. Mornings started early with breakfast, followed by group activities. Afternoons were reserved for individualized schedules, and the late afternoons brought free swim. Evenings culminated with everyone gathering on the field before heading to the mess hall for dinner. Each section had its own evening activity, and the counselors were left with the unenviable task of calming the kids and coaxing them into their bunks, hoping they were tired enough to avoid any after-lights-out mischief.

For the counselors, this was the best part of the day. They jokingly called it "Camp Hershey for Counselors" because, while the campers enjoyed their daily activities, the real fun happened at night for the staff. Except for the two staff members tasked with patrolling the field to ensure campers stayed in their cabins, the rest of the counselors would gather in small groups to unwind. Some played guitar and sang, others wandered into the woods for a quiet smoke, and many just hung out, forging friendships and creating memories that would last a lifetime.

Sam and Gregg, dressed in jeans and light sweatshirts to ward off the cool evening air, were in the mess hall playing cribbage. Two other counselors, who neither understood nor cared to learn the game, watched briefly as spectators. Sam dealt the cards, and both players tossed two into the crib.

"I've got chill kids," Gregg said, discarding a card and announcing, "Six."

Sam played a nine. "Fifteen for two," he said, moving his peg two holes forward. "I don't have to worry much about my cabin. Bill's got a good handle on them. I just help out where needed. Most of my responsibilities are around the lake during the day."

"Sailing a sunfish and sitting in a lifeguard chair during free swim must be exhausting," Gregg said with a grin, tossing a face card onto the table. "Twenty-five."

Sam smirked and played a six. "Thirty-one for two." He moved his peg again.

"You're crushing me," Gregg muttered as they gathered up the cards for the next hand. "Fifteen two, fifteen four, and a pair for six," he added while counting his hand.

One of the spectators shook his head. "I don't know what you guys are talking about with this game. We're out of here." He and his friend slid off the bench, grabbed their phones, and headed outside. Just as the door swung closed, Gina and Carrie Kellerman breezed in.

Unlike most of the other counselors, Gina and Carrie had taken the time to shower, change into clean clothes, and apply just enough makeup to highlight their features. Gina's long black hair cascaded down her back, while Carrie's blonde locks, almost as long, swayed over her shoulders. They paused just inside the door, scanning the room in synchronized movements. A breeze from the open window caused their hair to sway over their shoulders. Every male in the room glanced up, then quickly looked away, not wanting to be caught staring.

After a moment of silent appraisal, Gina and Carrie moved toward Sam and Gregg's table with the precision of predators stalking prey. Sam's palms grew clammy. He stared at his cards and threw down the two of clubs. "Seventeen."

Gregg glanced at his hand, the women now hovering beside the table. He discarded a nine. "Twenty-six." Neither man looked up.

"Can we join?" Gina asked, sliding onto the bench beside Sam without waiting for an answer. She gestured to her friend. "You remember Carrie? She's from Tennessee." Carrie wedged herself onto the bench next to Gregg, who shifted awkwardly to make room. The bench, designed for two campers, didn't provide much space for four adults. Gregg offered a nervous smile, his cheeks flushing.

"What're you playing?" Gina asked, squinting at Sam's cards.

"It's called cribbage," Sam replied. "My dad taught us when we were kids. It's easy to learn. Want to try?"

She smiled, her hand lightly brushing his arm. "Maybe we'll just watch for now." She pointed to Carrie. "We can pick it up by observing."

Over the next hour, Sam and Gregg played three games, explaining the rules as they went. Gina and Carrie eventually joined in for a round, laughing at their mistakes. Between turns, they exchanged tidbits about siblings, college, and their most embarrassing moments. Gina threw her head back in a full-throated laugh when Sam recounted how, during a ninth-grade biology presentation titled "Genetics and Heredity: Look at Your Parents, That's You in Thirty Years," he'd unknowingly delivered the entire talk with his zipper down.

"I killed it," Sam said with a rueful smile, "until Mark Lampenfield yelled, 'Kennywood's open!' Everyone cracked up, including my teacher. I didn't talk for the rest of the year."

Gina's gaze never left him as he told the story, nodding empathetically. When he finished, Carrie glanced at her phone. "It's late. My kids will be up before the sun."

Gina stood with her. "Goodnight. That was fun." Turning to Sam, she added in a low voice, "Let's hang out some more."

Sam nodded, too tongue-tied to respond. The two women sauntered out of the mess hall, their exit as striking as their entrance.

Gregg clapped Sam on the back. "They want to hang out with us more. This summer's shaping up to be excellent."

Sam's head bobbed in agreement as a wide grin spread across his face.

Chapter 7

Gregg's face was etched with concern, his eyes peering over a pile of legal documents in front of him. He kicked his feet onto Sam's desk and clasped his hands behind his head. For the past two hours, in between intermittent wisecracks and sharp personal jabs, they had been preparing his defense in the case where the woman he claimed he barely knew had accused him of harassment.

"It's all crap," Gregg said. "She has nothing, and the emails I have prove we were only talking—nothing lurid." He raised his eyebrows at Sam, as if daring him to disagree.

Sam shrugged. "You never know with cases like this. It's your word against hers. You told me she's articulate and should make a decent impression. She's filed in arbitration, so we've got limited discovery. We'll have to wing it."

"You're not instilling a lot of confidence in me." Gregg slumped a bit in his chair, his earlier bravado dimming.

Sam threw a balled-up piece of paper at Gregg, who watched it sail past his head. "Let's see how things develop. Meet me at my office at 8:30 on Wednesday. The hearing starts at 10:00. There will be three random lawyers acting as arbitrators. In my experience, that's the most important factor in these arbitrations—who gets assigned. If we get a bad panel, then the evidence doesn't matter." He blew out a frustrated breath. "Don't worry. You didn't do anything wrong. If you had, she'd be looking for much bigger damages."

Gregg glared at him. "She's just trying to get a quick payday. Luckily, I've got the best lawyer in town."

Sam waved dismissively. "Shucks, you city boys say the nicest things."

Gregg gathered his papers, but paused when Sam spoke again. "Before you go, guess who I heard from?"

Gregg shook his head. "Mrs. Columbo, our eleventh-grade English teacher? Big woman. Some of our more disturbed classmates called her Jumbo Columbo."

"No. Stop. So mean." Sam laughed, but then grew more serious. "Someone more important. Gina from Camp Hershey. Remember her?"

"No way. Hot Gina. Of course, I remember her. Though, to be honest, I remember her friend, Carrie, much better." He grinned mischievously.

"That's because you were hooking up with her all summer. Have you spoken to her since then?"

"No, but those were good times. I'm surprised she came back for a second summer, but that worked out pretty well, too. Wonder what she's doing now. Do you think she lays in bed and reminisces about those summers with me?"

Sam waved a hand in front of Gregg's face. "Hey, this is about me, not you. Gina, or as you so eloquently called her, 'Hot Gina,' reached out to me. Obviously because she's been pondering the time we spent together."

"Dude, you chased that woman for two summers. What do you have to show for all your efforts?"

"She loved me. She told me so many times. It may not have worked out quite the way I wanted, but we had a connection. You know it, and I know it."

Gregg laughed. "Carrie and I didn't have much of a connection. She was dumber than a rock, but she was fun. Never worried about commitments. I'll never forget some of the places she took me at night at that camp."

"But Gina and I had something deeper. We talked for hours. I learned everything about her life. She told me how special our friendship was."

"Emphasis on the word 'friendship.'"

"You mock, but you know we had something going on."

"The only person she had something going on with was Trevor Morrison. She wasn't just friends with him."

Sam winced. "Don't mention that name. I still get hives when I think about him." He raised his eyebrows. "But she reached out to me. I'm sure she still feels the connection."

"Sure, she does." Gregg stood and picked up the stack of documents. "I think you should focus on getting Jenny back. Gina was a long time ago. Hopefully, you learned some lessons."

Sam reached out a fist for Gregg to bump. "Maybe I can get Jenny back, and maybe I can reconnect with Gina. Best of both worlds."

Gregg scoffed. "Sounds like the kind of thinking that got you into trouble in the first place." He turned to leave but paused at the doorway. "Be careful," he said, seeming to want to add more, but instead walked out of the office.

Chapter 8

*T*REVOR MORRISON ALWAYS SEEMED *at ease, like every-thing came without effort. He moved with a confident stride, his long brown hair bouncing with every step, creating the illusion that he was untroubled by the stressors that weighed down ordinary mortals—no sleepless nights fretting over final exams or unrequited crushes.*

On the first night of camp, after the rest of the staff had already gone through icebreakers, Trevor arrived fashionably late. His car tore down the dirt road, leaving a trail of dust behind. When he finally pulled up in his faded, metallic green Chevy, there was no trace of tension or awkwardness—just the effortless poise of the "cool kid" making an entrance. Despite not knowing anyone, he was chatting with the camp director and other counselors within minutes, as though he'd been part of the team for years.

Trevor was assigned to teach archery, even though he'd never held a bow or arrow before. After just a couple of days of practice, he became the camp's most proficient archer. Though he held no strong opinions on kids handling weapons, he quickly established safety protocols for the archery range, reducing the risk of accidents. Remarkably, those protocols are still in use today.

During his first nights at camp, Trevor joined a group of counselors for impromptu guitar jam sessions. Some were skilled musicians, having studied music in college; others ranged from those with basic training to amateurs like Trevor, who could strum a few chords but tried to look convincing to the untrained eye. With his rudimentary skills, Trevor managed to bang out old classics from James Taylor to Harry Chapin, fitting in reasonably well.

The jam sessions, held around one of the long tables in the mess hall, attracted others who joined in to sing along. When the tempo picked up, Trevor would smack the base of his guitar to create a beat, inspiring rhythmic clapping from the group. As the music grew more intense, Trevor's head bobbed in time, his hair falling over his eyes. He'd flick it away with a practiced gesture, but it inevitably tumbled back, much to the amusement—and interest—of the women watching him.

Sam, Gregg, Gina, and Carrie often hung out together after dark. The previous evening, Gregg and Carrie had suddenly left early, leaving Sam and Gina alone to play cards. Sam didn't mind the one-on-one time. In fact, he welcomed it. Tonight, when Gregg mentioned heading out with Carrie again, Sam felt a spark of hope.

Sam relished the growing closeness with Gina. She confided in him, and he listened, mindful of his father's advice: "It's better to listen than to talk." Over the past few nights, she'd shared her summer goals—to perfect her tan, read as much as possible, run each morning before the campers woke, and, most intriguingly, find a special guy.

Gina had also recounted her entire dating history, from the awkward prom date who became her high school boyfriend and took her virginity on graduation night, to the flings of freshman year, the "dry spell" during second term when she prioritized sorority friendships, and the senior who broke things off after graduation to avoid "strings attached."

"I thought we might keep it going, even after he graduated," she had told Sam the night before. "But apparently not. I like having a steady relationship—and lots of sex. I'm keeping my options open this summer."

Sam couldn't stop replaying her words in his head. "Lots of sex" echoed incessantly, especially when he saw her at the lake earlier that day, her tight shorts and bikini top sparking his imagination. He hoped she had been hinting at him—or at least saw him as a contender.

Sam was determined to escape the dreaded friend zone. He'd spent too much of his high school and college years stuck there, where girls liked him but never seemed to want more. Tonight, he vowed to be bolder, more direct, to show Gina there was more to him than just being a good listener.

The four friends sat around a small table, cards forgotten in a pile. They'd been chatting for hours, the strumming of guitars and faint chirping of crickets filling the background.

"I'm getting stiff sitting here," Gregg said, rubbing his legs.

"Same," Carrie replied, smiling at him.

Gregg nodded. "Let's take a walk."

Before anyone could respond, the pair was already heading for the door. The squeak of the coiled wire of the screen door signaled its opening and the thwack of it hitting the wooden frame marked its closing, leaving Sam and Gina alone at the table.

Sam stretched, smiling at her. "My legs could use some movement, too."

Gina nodded. "You're right. Maybe we should do something else."

Sam stood, but she didn't, instead turning her head towards the guitar players. "Let's join them. It looks like fun."

Along with having to clean out the stables, this was among the last items on his list of things he wanted to do at that moment. He hated to sing, he didn't know many of the lyrics, and had hoped for something more intimate.

With the rhythms of the guitarists filling the space, Gina sauntered over to the music and came alive. Within moments, she had eased herself into Trevor's line of sight. She sang, clapped, and swayed her hips in time with the beat. Trevor noticed. He lifted his gaze from his guitar to meet hers, biting his lower lip in a way Sam was sure he'd practiced for hours in front of a mirror.

Sam's stomach dropped. He could see it unfolding, yet felt powerless to stop it. Blood rushed to his head, leaving him dizzy and helpless as Gina tilted her head, smiled at Trevor, and blushed when he glanced her way.

After the song ended, Trevor muttered something to the group and headed for the door, tossing Gina a brief look before leaving. She followed moments later, slipping out as discreetly as a mouse.

Sam stood frozen, his heart pounding and his face pale. After another song, he trudged out of the mess hall. He stormed up the path to his cabin, fists clenched. His emotions warred between anger and heartbreak. He stopped underneath a towering pine tree, wiped his face with his sleeve, and entered his bunk, alone.

Chapter 9

WITH HIS FEET KICKED up on his desk, Sam leaned back in his chair, his phone held in front of his face. He had already rehearsed what he'd say if one of the partners walked into his office: "Just talking with a potential new client. Bad injury. Hope they're going to sign up next week."

He was stoked. Gina had agreed to a phone call so they were about to talk. No more waiting three minutes for a reply. Her voice would be in his ear.

Now was the perfect time. Her husband was at work, and she had a late hospital shift. Sure, he had briefs to write and discovery to answer, but this was far more important.

His palms were sweaty as he punched in the number.

She picked up before the second ring. "Hey, I'm so glad you called." Her voice was the same as it had been fifteen years ago—a little raspy, a lot sexy. The sound swept him back to Camp Hershey. He could almost smell the grass.

"I'm glad I called, too."

"How are you?"

"I'm good. This is so weird."

She giggled. "I know. But I really wanted to talk to you."

"Why?"

"I have so much to say. Texting's been fun. We've been doing it a lot, and it's so easy to talk to you, even that way. But that's no surprise. You were always my favorite person to talk to."

"I liked talking to you, too."

"Thanks. I also wanted to apologize for how I treated you back at camp."

"What do you mean?"

"I feel like I led you on. I wanted to let you know I had very strong feelings for you back then. I was silly and couldn't see what was in front of me."

"You didn't do anything wrong."

"Yes, I did. And I want to make it up to you."

"Really?" Sam's heart beat faster.

"Of course. I can't believe how easily we've gotten back to where we were before. It feels so right. I never get that feeling when I talk with my husband. It's so different with him."

"Why?"

"I don't know. Our marriage seems to be falling apart. We never see each other."

He wanted to skip around the room. "What do you mean?"

She giggled some more. "I'm looking for something more."

"Tell me!"

A noise came through the phone. "Damn, Pablo just got home. Must be some problem at work. I gotta go. Can we talk more later?"

"Absolutely."

The call disconnected. She was gone, at least for now. Sam exhaled deeply and leaned back in his chair with her words replaying in his head. He realized he longed for much more.

The sun hung high in the sky, casting light onto the green grass of the baseball field, which had been trampled all summer and deserved a winter of rest. The staff stood almost motionless as the last car pulled out of the gate. The campers were gone, and within a few hours, the camp would be left to the maintenance crew until the following year.

The rituals of summer were coming to an end. Most of the staff wrestled with the difficulties of saying goodbye to new and old friends while facing the reality of returning home. They sensed the long-term impact these relationships would have on their lives but were already transitioning their thoughts back to family and friends they hadn't seen in months.

Sam and Gregg sat on the grass, resting after loading gear into cars for hours. Mixed emotions ruled the day. Parents were thrilled to hug their kids, but both campers and parents would miss the independence summer camp provided. Not until next year would the kids have the same freedom to roam and explore. The adults would miss the quiet and solitude soon to vanish once their kids returned home.

Neither spoke at first, leaning back to catch the last rays of summer. After a few minutes, Sam turned to Gregg. "What did you decide to do about your 'situation'?" His words floated into the warm air.

Gregg laughed. "Nothing needed to be done. Carrie and I agreed to end everything before we left. She's going back to Vandy. We won't be within two hundred miles of each other. It was awesome while it lasted. We capped it off last night, but we're not talking anymore. She doesn't want any strings. Neither do I. Clean break." He sat up. "Have you talked to her?" He emphasized the word 'her.'

Sam chuckled, about to respond, but Gina plopped onto the ground next to him. She threw her arm around his shoulders. "Just wanted to say goodbye. It was an amazing summer. So glad we became friends. You have my contact info. Keep in touch." She leaned over and kissed Sam on the cheek, then hugged Gregg. "Bye, boys. Hopefully, we'll all be back next year." She jumped to her feet and ran to the group by the basketball court.

"I guess that answers your question," Sam said, shaking his head. "She spent all summer with Trevor. I had to watch them every day."

"You compensated fine."

He scoffed. "A couple of flings. Big deal. I didn't care. Never stopped thinking about her."

"You won't have to worry about running into her anymore. She'll be hanging out at her party school. Can only imagine the trouble she'll be causing."

"True." Sam stood. "I guess it's time for us to head out." They bro-hugged. "See you back at home." He walked toward his car.

"Don't worry. You'll forget about her. I'll make sure of it," Gregg called out.

Sam raised a fist over his head but didn't turn back.

Chapter 10

O NE OF THE MOST *alluring aspects of returning to camp each year is the sense of stepping into a time warp. Nothing much changes. The cabins look the same, the food is as predictable as ever, and the overall experience retains its familiar rhythm. For many returnees, this sameness is exactly what they crave—comforting consistency paired with opportunities for new adventures.*

Sam chose to come back for a second summer for a few reasons. First, he had nothing better to do. Sophomore year had been tough, and he was looking forward to a break from the mental strain. A relaxing summer overseeing the beachfront seemed like the perfect reprieve before diving back into his studies in the fall.

Gregg, on the other hand, had committed early and secured a small pay bump by agreeing to be a section head. He suspected this would be his final year at camp and vowed to enjoy his evenings as much as humanly possible.

When Gregg learned Sam was wavering on his decision to return, he reached out to Carrie, who mentioned that both she and Gina would be back. This news only deepened Sam's uncertainty. However, it wasn't until he discovered that Trevor Morrison would be leading a youth trip to explore the Australian Outback that Sam finally made up his mind to return.

So far, his summer had been fine. The lake had become his personal sanctuary, and the kids' boundless enthusiasm kept his days lively. His tan deepened under the relentless sun, and he relished being seen as one of the camp leaders. Wherever he went, kids clung to him—piggy-backing up Hawkeye Path, shouting for more when he put them down, or eagerly following him to their next activity.

Yet, despite the outward appearance of contentment, Sam wrestled with inner turmoil. He and Gina spoke often, but there was no spark between them. The only person who truly understood his predicament was Gregg, who frequently encouraged him to look elsewhere. "There's plenty of talent here," Gregg teased, but Sam remained oblivious to anyone other than Gina.

Still, Sam clung to hope. "She hasn't hooked up with anyone else, as far as I know," he told Gregg one evening. Gregg offered a supportive smile. "Then make your move. Maybe she's just waiting for you."

That night, under a sky brimming with stars, the air cooled as Sam spotted Gina sitting alone on a stump, gazing up at the heavens, lost in thought.

"They're incredible, aren't they?" Sam said as he approached. "Sometimes it's overwhelming to take them all in. It helps to focus on a few at a time." He pointed to a bright cluster in the northern sky. "That's Cassiopeia. See the 'W'? In Greek mythology, she was a vain and imperious queen who angered the gods."

Gina's lips curved into a small smile. "How do you know that?"

"My dad used to take us camping. He loved pointing out constellations. I thought it was fascinating as a kid, imagining tiny people living on the stars, waiting for me to visit them."

She let out a small laugh and reached over to touch his arm. "That's adorable. Show me more." Her finger traced upward, but her eyes stayed on him.

He scanned the sky. "That's Scorpius," he said, gesturing to a string of shimmering lights. "He was Orion's nemesis. They chase each other across the sky, season after season, forever."

"That's amazing. I only know the Big Dipper. You're full of surprises." She touched his arm again, her voice warm.

Sam hesitated, then said, "You can see even better from the lake." He bit his lower lip. "Want to go?"

Everyone knew what an invitation to the lake after dark meant. Sam waited, his wide eyes betraying his nervousness.

Gina lowered her gaze, but nodded. "Sure, that sounds fun."

They walked down the grassy path, following the shoreline until they reached a secluded patch known as "the cove." The soft sand muffled their steps, and moonlight glinted on the water's surface. Sam found a blanket among the supplies stashed under the rocks and spread it out. They sat side by side, quietly watching the lake.

When Gina shivered, Sam handed her his hoodie. She slipped it on and nestled closer to him.

"Do you want to talk more about the stars?" he asked in a whisper.

She shook her head and leaned in until their lips met. Her kiss was soft, tentative, but quickly deepened. He pulled her close, desiring to feel every part of her next to him, his body alive with desire.

He started to kiss her neck, and her head tilted back as she grabbed his hair. But as he moved forward to lie beside her, Gina's hands pressed firmly against his chest. Startled, he pulled back.

"What's wrong?" he asked, his voice heavy with confusion.

Gina turned away, hugging her knees. "I can't," she said, almost in a whisper. "It's not that I don't want to. I just. . .can't."

"Did I do something wrong?" he asked, his throat tight.

She shook her head. "It's not you." She wavered. "I just don't want to ruin our friendship. It means too much to me."

Sam felt his chest tighten as rejection washed over him. "I thought you wanted this."

"You didn't misread me," she said, tears glistening in her eyes. "But I'm not in a good place right now. I can't do this to you."

Before he could respond, she jumped to her feet. She opened her mouth as if to say more, but then turned and ran.

Sam chased her partway up the path before stopping. He returned to the stump where they'd first spoken, but Gina was nowhere to be found. Looking up, he spotted Scorpius, glittering in the sky. His chin fell to his chest, and he exhaled a weak breath. Like Scorpius forever pursuing Orion, he realized he might be chasing Gina for eternity.

Chapter 11

---

*G*REGG SPLASHED A PAIR *of nine-year-old campers, who were two feet shorter than him. He had no difficulty handling the weak dribbles the kids managed to launch his way. Like Godzilla in Tokyo, he lurched toward them, undeterred by their flailing attempts at resistance. The two boys braced themselves as he approached, pounding his chest and slapping at the water in mock defiance.*

He grabbed one boy, skinny as a rail and sporting a set of oversized swimming goggles. Lifting him high overhead, Gregg extended his arms and roared, "This is for splashing me and interrupting my rest hour. You shall be punished!" He spun slowly in circles, searching for the perfect spot to toss the boy, whose uncontrolled laughter echoed across the lake.

A sharp whistle cut through the air. Everyone froze and turned toward the lifeguard stand, where Sam stood waving. "Put the child down," he shouted. "This is the third time I've had to warn you about breaking the rules." Sam shook his head and threw his thumb over his shoulder. "Out of the water. Ten-minute break."

All summer long, the camp had been emphasizing strict rule enforcement to prioritize safety. Sam didn't mind Gregg's antics, but he knew that making an example of him in front of the campers might prevent future rule-breaking.

Gregg sighed dramatically, lowered the boy to his feet, and patted his head. Then, with his lower lip jutting out in exaggerated sulkiness, he trudged out of the water and made his way over to Sam. The lake's surface rippled again as everyone resumed their activities.

"Thanks, dude," Gregg said as he approached. "You got me out of the water. I needed a break anyway."

"Not a problem," Sam replied, keeping his eyes on the swimmers.

"Mind if I sit here for my timeout?" Gregg spread out his towel and plopped down at the base of the lifeguard chair.

"Make yourself at home," Sam said without turning his head.

For a few minutes, neither spoke. Gregg leaned back, soaking in the sun, until he broke the silence. "Gina's over there," he said, nodding toward a group of swimmers. "Have you talked to her lately? Only a week left."

Sam shook his head. "We've talked, but nothing like we used to have. No mention of what happened at the lake. It's all small talk. 'Hey, how are you?' 'Warm day, isn't it?' That's as far as it goes."

"That's rough. She was like hit and run with you. That was weeks ago."

"Yeah. She'll come over, smile at me, but the second I try to start a real conversation, she's gone. It's like she doesn't want to engage."

"So, what are you going to do about it?"

Sam shrugged. "Not sure there's much I can do. I want to take her back to the cove, just the two of us, to see if there's still a connection. I know if we could talk, really talk, she'd remember what we had."

"I'm wishing you luck, but you're missing out on a lot." Gregg gestured toward the water. "Look at all that. Two-piece swimsuits in every color imaginable, but you're stuck on one girl in a pink suit. Live a little these last few days."

"I haven't had much fun all summer. Why start now? I'm a one-flavor kind of guy. Not interested in anyone else."

"You're blowing your summer," Gregg said, standing and brushing off his towel. "If I were you, I'd reconsider. Anyway, is my punishment over? Can I go back in? Carrie's over there, and I want to mess around, even if you're determined to mope."

Sam sighed and waved him off. "Go ahead. You've served your time. Have a blast."

Gregg high-stepped it back into the lake, diving underwater. Moments later, he resurfaced with Carrie's leg in his hand. She squealed and splashed at him as he grabbed her other leg and lifted her out of the water. With a dramatic spin, he tossed her back in, her laughter ringing out.

From his perch, Sam watched the scene unfold. He raised his whistle, ready to intervene, but hesitated. Lowering the whistle, he shook his head and smirked. *That boy will never grow up,* he thought.

Chapter 12

SAM ARRIVED AT HIS office early, determined to ensure everything was in place for Gregg's arbitration. He meticulously reviewed his files, confirming that all exhibits were pre-marked and witness outlines were ready. Satisfied, he allowed himself a moment to relax before Gregg's arrival. With extra time to spare, Sam decided to see if Gina was available for a quick chat. His nerves spiking, he starting tapping on his phone.

> Hey, what's up? Can you chat for a few?

> Of course. I've enjoyed our chats so far. It's been so nice catching up.

> You're very kind.

> My amazing husband is here getting dressed, so I don't have much time.

Sam appreciated the heads-up.

What are you doing today?

I've got work this afternoon—late shift.

Always doing important work.

Thanks, both of us try. How about you?

Helping a friend with an arbitration today.
Lots of work piled up for the afternoon.

You're a busy attorney. Impressive.

Thanks.

Hey, Pablo and I are going to have some
breakfast. Take care.

And just like that, she was gone. Mentioning her husband's
name felt like a gut punch, and Sam bristled at how flat their
exchange had been compared to past conversations. Still, there
wasn't much he could do about it. He consoled himself with the
hope that their next chat might have a bit more spark.

His brooding was interrupted by an email notification: Gregg
had arrived and was on his way up. Moments later, he appeared in
the doorway, dressed in a suit, his hair neatly combed.

"You showed up just when I was texting Gina," Sam said with a grin. "It was just starting to get interesting, and now I have to deal with you." He gave Gregg a friendly slap on the back. "But it's great to see you."

Gregg chuckled, shaking his head. "Thanks. . .I think. We've done a lot of prep, but can you run me through the basics one more time? I know I've been in court a lot, but this feels like my first day."

Sam gestured to the chair opposite his desk and sat down. "Sure thing, buddy. We're ready, but a quick review never hurts. Let's go over a few key points before we head out."

"You're in charge. Just walk me through it again, step by step."

"We'll head across the street to the courthouse," Sam began. "For arbitration, there will be two rooms, each with three lawyers acting as arbitrators for the day. They get paid the same whether the session lasts an hour or eight, so they appreciate it when presentations are concise. We won't know who the arbitrators are until we step into the room."

Gregg frowned. "That sounds a little ominous."

"Not at all," Sam reassured him. "This is routine. The key is not to overthink who we'll face. We focus on presenting the facts, which are in our favor, and we stay unemotional."

"Got it. So, I just let you take the lead and stay calm?"

"Exactly. If anyone gets argumentative, that's my job. When it's your turn to testify, you stay professional. Your answers should be consistent no matter how much they press you."

Gregg nodded but glanced up at the ceiling, visibly uneasy. "Dude, I have to admit—I'm a little nervous."

"That's normal," Sam said. "You're used to being in control, and this process is unpredictable. I could tell you not to worry, but you will—at least until we get the decision."

Gregg smirked. "Funny. I tell my clients the same thing. Most of them end up in jail."

"That's the difference between civil and criminal defense," Sam replied with a grin. "When I lose a case, my clients can come find me later. When you lose, your clients are hauled out of the courtroom in shackles."

Gregg laughed. "I hadn't thought of it that way. You civil attorneys have a clear advantage."

Sam stood, grabbing his briefcase. "Let's go find out if you'll have a reason to be mad at me later."

Chapter 13

THE ARBITRATION HOLDING ROOM was all too familiar to Sam. He had spent countless mornings there, waiting for hearings to begin. Working at a small firm often meant handling routine cases, many of which were resolved in this very room. The cases here were typically characterized by truncated opening statements, concise testimony, and swift outcomes—all aimed at keeping client expenses manageable when disputes involved smaller sums of money. Gregg sat beside Sam, fidgeting with his hands while scanning the room. Lawyers huddled with their clients, poring over documents, while a few individuals stood alone, likely unwilling to hire legal representation for their cases.

Shortly after 10 a.m., a stocky man in a short-sleeved dress shirt entered the room, carrying a banker's box. Without a word, he set it on a desk, wiped his glistening forehead with a handkerchief, and began pulling out a stack of folders, which he unceremoniously dumped out. A line formed in front of him, and for the next ten minutes, all parties checked in.

Once the check-in process was complete, the clerk bellowed, *"Armond v. Simmons*. You're in room one!" Two lawyers—one in a gray suit, the other in navy—accompanied by their clients, waddled down the hallway.

"We're next," Sam said. Almost on cue, the clerk called out, "*Chokra v. Hubbard*, please follow me."

Sam grabbed his briefcase, motioned for Gregg to follow, and walked down the hallway. Trailing them were a young woman in a professional pantsuit and another woman in a form-fitting, less professional outfit. Sam surmised the first was the opposing attorney and introduced himself before entering the arbitration room.

Inside, the parties took their places. Sam opened his folder and began organizing his exhibits while his counterpart did the same. At the front of the room, three arbitrators sat behind a long desk. The youngest—a petite woman whose suit sleeves extended slightly too far down her arms—stood and announced, "All those who will be testifying, please rise and repeat after me." Gregg and the woman in the revealing outfit stood, and after a brief oath, both affirmed they would tell the truth.

The senior arbitrator, seated at the center, spoke next. "We've reviewed the case materials and have a general understanding of the claims. Let's begin with brief opening statements, followed by testimony."

The opposing attorney flipped to the front page of her yellow legal pad. "Good morning. My name is Gretchen Tallon, and I represent Amy Chokra in her claim against Gregory Hubbard. Mr. Hubbard and Ms. Chokra were members of Silver's Gym downtown. They used to work out there, often at the same time. On multiple occasions, Mr. Hubbard asked Ms. Chokra out, despite her repeated refusals. Eventually, she agreed to go to lunch, hoping it would put an end to his advances.

"At this lunch, Ms. Chokra made it clear she wasn't interested in dating him. Unfortunately, Mr. Hubbard didn't accept this and continued harassing her—at the gym and beyond. This behavior forced Ms. Chokra to quit the gym and seek counseling. Her psychologist diagnosed her with post-traumatic stress disorder. She continues to receive treatment to this day.

"Mr. Hubbard's actions constitute harassment, causing significant emotional damage to my client. We seek compensation for these damages. Thank you." She sat down, leaning back in her chair.

The senior arbitrator nodded to Sam, who stood and spoke without referring to his notes. "Gregg Hubbard engaged in no behavior that could be construed as harassment. He and Ms. Chokra met at the gym and developed a casual friendship. They had lunch once—an uneventful meeting—and saw each other a few more times before Ms. Chokra abruptly disappeared from the gym. The claims of harassment are unfounded and lack any supporting evidence. We will seek a decision in Mr. Hubbard's favor."

Sam sat.

The arbitrator turned to Ms. Tallon. "Call your first witness."

"The plaintiff calls Amy Chokra."

Chokra took a seat in the makeshift witness stand. She wore a cream-colored blouse that hugged her athletic frame underneath a tight fitting jacket, a testament to her continued fitness routine despite no longer frequenting Silver's Gym.

"Please introduce yourself to the arbitrators," Tallon began.

"My name is Amy Chokra. I'm a registered nurse in the maternity ward at Memorial General Hospital."

"Did you use the facilities at Silver's Gym?"

"I did. I was a member for over three years and liked to take classes or lift weights after work. Now, I go elsewhere."

Tallon nodded. "How did you meet Mr. Hubbard?" She tossed her hand in Gregg's direction.

"We worked out at the same time. One day, he approached me and asked if I wanted to lift weights together."

"And did you?"

"Yes. It's safer to have a spotter."

"Did your interactions progress beyond the gym?"

"I wouldn't call it a relationship. We worked out together a few times. He asked me out occasionally, but I thought he was joking and always said no. Eventually, he asked me to lunch."

"And you agreed?"

"I did. I thought a public lunch would be safe. After a workout, we went to a nearby sandwich shop. It was casual and brief."

"Did you feel any connection with him?"

"No. He seemed nice enough, but I wasn't interested."

"Was he interested in you?"

"Yes. At lunch, he asked me out repeatedly for the weekend. When I declined, he seemed irritated but then regained his composure. After that, I started feeling uncomfortable around him at the gym."

"Did he contact you outside the gym?"

"Yes. He somehow got my number. I don't know how, but he would text me some disgusting things, like how good I would look with my clothes off or how he knew that I liked it rough."

"Did you save the messages?"

"No. He used an app that made them disappear after I read them. I wish I realized they had some encryption, and I would have taken a screen shot, or done something to save them."

"What did the messages say?"

Sam stood. "Objection. Hearsay and violation of the best evidence rule."

The middle arbitrator thought for a moment. "I don't believe they are offering the texts for the truth of the statements contained in them, but for the plaintiff's reaction to them." He looked at counsel. "Am I correct?"

"You are," she said.

"Then the objection is overruled. Proceed."

Tallon turned back to her client. "What did the texts say?"

"A bunch of awful stuff. Like, 'Don't you think we should hook up?' and 'I think you're smoking hot.' He once said how sexy I look in my workout clothes and how he bet I would look sexier without them. Things like that."

"How many of these texts did you get from Mr. Hubbard?"

"Dozens. For over a week. I begged him to stop, but he didn't."

"And then what did you do?"

"I waited for him one day outside the gym. When I saw him, I calmly approached and told him that if he didn't stop texting me, I would get the police involved."

"Did he respond in any way?"

"He just leered at me and refused to acknowledge I was speaking. I felt so vulnerable that I began to shake. So, I went to the front desk and quit. I informed them about what he had done. Do you know their response? 'It's a gym. It happens all the time.'"

"Did Mr. Hubbard do anything after that?"

Chokra nodded. "He did. He started showing up at my apartment. He would buzz from downstairs, but I wouldn't let him in. It freaked me out."

"So, how has it been since then?"

"After about a week, he finally decided to leave me alone. I haven't seen or heard from him since. I'm relieveCd about that, but his stalking messed me up. When I would return to my place, I felt unsafe, like the walls were closing in on me."

Chokra pulled a tissue from he jacket pocket. "I made an appointment with a therapist and have been seeing her weekly to discuss the situation. She's been helping me work through the trust issues I never had before all this."

Tallon stood, picked up a pile of papers, and handed a set to Sam before distributing copies to the arbitrators. "These are the plaintiff's medical records, her treatment bills, and the expert report of Dr. Imohye, her psychiatrist. As you can see, Dr. Imohye concludes that Mr. Hubbard's conduct was harassing and directly led to Ms.

Chokra's need for therapy. He also states she will require further treatment in the future."

She sat down. "How are you now, Ms. Chokra?"

"I'm doing a lot better. I'm still cautious around men, and I haven't dated at all. But with some support, I think I'll be ready to try again."

"Thank you. I don't have any more questions."

Sam turned toward the witness and flipped a page on his yellow pad. "Ma'am, you say Mr. Hubbard harassed you and texted you constantly."

"He did," she replied, crossing her arms.

"Yet, other than your word, you haven't brought one shred of evidence with you today, have you?"

"I couldn't. His messages just disappeared."

"And you don't have screenshots of those alleged texts, do you?"

"I don't. I didn't realize I'd need them before they were gone."

"You don't have evidence of anything, do you? You don't even have a receipt for the lunch you claim the two of you had."

"I don't. Again, I didn't think about saving it at the time."

"You don't have witnesses to corroborate your version of these events, do you?"

"I usually don't have someone reading over my shoulder when I open a text."

"And no one at the gym can confirm that Gregg made the statements you're accusing him of making?"

"No."

"Nor do you have friends who saw the texts or who can verify you complained of being harassed at the time?"

"No."

Sam stared at her. "So, without any additional proof, it's your word against his?"

She nodded, but didn't respond verbally.

"Finally, regarding your claimed injuries, isn't it true you sought treatment from a psychologist long before seeing Dr. Imohye?"

She hesitated. "That was years ago, for very personal reasons."

He raised an eyebrow and pulled out a folder. "Please confirm these are your records from a psychologist, Dr. Andrews."

He handed her the documents. She skimmed through them. "Yes, these are my personal medical records with Dr. Andrews."

"Please turn to the tabbed page. I have two questions for you."

She complied.

"Isn't it true Dr. Andrews, long before you met Mr. Hubbard, diagnosed you with post-traumatic stress disorder?"

She couldn't argue with what was on the papers. "Yes."

"And wasn't that after a different boyfriend had broken up with you.?"

Her gaze didn't leave the documents. "Yes."

"I have no further questions." Sam turned to Gregg, who offered a supportive smile and a brief pat on the back.

The lead arbitrator glanced at Tallon. "Do you have any more witnesses or evidence?"

Tallon said, "Plaintiff rests."

"Then it's the defendant's turn."

Sam stood. "Defendant calls Gregg Hubbard."

Gregg walked to the witness chair and signaled his readiness.

"Tell the arbitrators your name and occupation."

"My name is Gregg Hubbard. I'm a criminal defense attorney."

"Where do you work?"

"I work in a small firm with a couple of other lawyers."

"Do you know the plaintiff?"

Gregg nodded. "I do. We met at Silver's Gym."

"How well do you know her?"

"Not that well. At the gym, it's common to partner with someone. We did that a few times. So, I got to know her name and a little about her. Not much more. I guess I would call us workout buddies.'" He offered a weak smile.

"Did you ever go to lunch with her?"

"Yes, once. She suggested we grab something to eat after a workout. I agreed."

"What happened?"

"Not much. We got some sandwiches, talked about work, and then I left."

"Did either of you ask the other out after the lunch?"

"No."

"Did she ask you out again?"

"No."

"Did you see her again?"

"A few times at the gym. Then she disappeared. I didn't think much of it until I got served with her complaint."

"Did you and she ever text?"

"She texted a couple of times asking if I was going to the gym. I told her when I would be there."

"Did you ever message her on a secret, disappearing app?"

He scoffed. "No. I didn't even know those existed."

Sam handed a small stack of papers to the arbitrators. "These are copies of all the texts between them. As you can see, they are few and innocuous."

He returned to his seat. "I have no further questions."

Tallon's questioning of Gregg was brief. He again denied asking out Chokra and sending her texts which soon disappeared. He grimaced when she suggested he had harassed her and stated without emotion, he had never done anything close to harassing her or anyone else.

Tallon had nothing on Gregg, and he gave her no space to press him. Tallon realized pressing further would yield no results and sat down, clearly frustrated.

Sam informed the arbitrators the defense had no further witnesses or evidence. The lead arbitrator confirmed they had heard the evidence and dismissed the need for closing statements. He asked the parties to wait outside for the decision.

"That was anti-climactic," Gregg sighed as they exited.

"Let's see what they decide before jumping to conclusions," Sam advised once they were alone.

Chapter 14

LITTLE NOOKS AND DUSTY crannies dotted the edges of the long hallway outside the arbitration room, making it easy for Sam and Gregg to find a secluded spot to wait for the arbitrators' decision. Gregg leaned back in a small wooden chair, his head tilted over the edge.

"I hope they believe me," he murmured.

Sam smiled to offer reassurance. "No reason they shouldn't. She didn't have any evidence—just her word, and frankly, I doubt that counts for much."

"It's insane where this is coming from," Gregg said, shaking his head. "She just up and left, and now I'm the one getting sued." He smacked Sam's knee. "Thanks for helping me out here. If I'd handled this alone, I might've strangled her."

"You demonstrated remarkable restraint in there," Sam replied, returning the smack on Gregg's leg.

"Maybe once we're outside, I'll tell her what I really think." Gregg smirked. "No, seriously, you saved my ass. If you ever need help, I'm here for you."

Sam waved him off. "Let's just send the arbitrators some positive vibes so they come to the right decision." Before they could continue, the younger arbitrator stepped into the hallway and called everyone back inside. Sam and Gregg exchanged a glance and shrugged.

"Guess it's time to find out," Sam said. They rose from their chairs and headed back to get the decision.

Inside the room, Gregg avoided looking at the plaintiff as the participants returned to their seats. The lead arbitrator cleared her throat, commanding everyone's attention.

"Thank you all for your efficient and effective presentations," she began. "Both parties have been ably represented. As this is an arbitration, we only announce the result—we do not provide the reasoning behind our decision." She glanced at her yellow notepad. "The panel has unanimously found in favor of the defendant, Greggory Hubbard."

The announcement landed without much reaction. Gregg placed a firm hand on Sam's shoulder and gave it a squeeze. Sam turned to shake the opposing attorney's hand in silence.

Outside the room, the parties parted ways without interaction. Once in the hallway, Sam pulled Gregg aside.

"Congratulations," Sam said. "I think the arbitrators saw through her story. No evidence, no credibility—it's as simple as that."

Gregg offered a strained smile, but it didn't reach his eyes. "I spent my morning in court just to break even after she dragged my name through the mud. Doesn't feel like much of a victory."

"It could've been worse," Sam said with a shrug. "Nowadays, we all have to be careful—social situations, social media. Anything you say can come back to haunt you someday."

As they walked toward the elevators, Gregg glanced at Sam, his eyes wide. "Maybe this is a wake-up call. I'm a single guy—this could happen again. We've got to be mindful of stuff our parents never had to think about. Honestly, I wish I were in a stable relationship so I wouldn't have to worry about every little thing I say."

Sam shot him a knowing, ironic look. "You and me both."

Chapter 15

A T FOUR YEARS OLD, Nathan brimmed with energy, racing through life with an almost perpetual smile. His hands grazed everything in his path—tables, food, people. At this age, most found his curiosity endearing, but Sam couldn't help but wonder how much longer its charm would last.

The playground buzzed with kids climbing ladders, darting through gates, and burning off their boundless energy on a bright Saturday afternoon. Nathan's reddish-blond hair flopped into his eyes with every movement, forcing him to shake his head to see better. He needed a haircut.

Taking Nathan to the park had once been a cherished ritual for Sam and Jenny, a time to hold hands while walking or sitting together on a bench, watching their son explore his world. Sure, they kept an eye out to ensure he played well with other children, but it was also a chance to steal moments for themselves.

Lately, though, these outings had become chores rather than shared pleasures. Parenting felt more like a task to complete than a joy to share. Even their home life had shifted. Cooking, once a shared passion, had turned into drudgery. DIY projects they used to tackle as a team were now done solo because "it's more efficient that way." Their conversations revolved around parenting logistics, not the dreams they once shared about building a life together.

Minor disagreements over dinner plans left tiny residual wounds which lingered, still exposed in the mornings. Disagreements over what Nathan should wear for cold weather morphed into evenings of silence which stretched into weeks without intimacy. It all built up, one small wound at a time, until one night Jenny exploded. "I can't even stand to look at your face anymore!" she screamed.

Now, Sam sat alone on a park bench, one arm draped over the backrest, reflecting on the collapse of their marriage. The sun warmed his face, dulling a minute portion of his misery.

How cliché, he thought. They weren't the first couple in their friend group to fall apart after having kids. Everyone knew life would change with children, but few were truly ready to confront how profound those changes could be.

Nathan at least, seemed unaffected—for now. He was the same whirlwind of energy, sprinting in circles, tumbling to the ground, and laughing as he popped back up to do it all over again. Sam couldn't yet grasp what long-term effects their split might have on his son, but the uncertainty gnawed at him.

Leaning back, Sam closed his eyes, his body sinking into the bench. Just as he teetered on the edge of a semi-nap, Nathan appeared out of nowhere and slapped his leg. The playful hit startled Sam back into the present.

"Daddy, chase me!" Nathan's dirt-smudged face beamed with excitement, his eyes wide with anticipation.

A light breeze tousled Sam's hair as he grinned at his son. He let out a playful growl. "You better run, or I'm going to eat you!" Raising his arms to imitate a ghoulish monster, he wiggled his fingers like he was playing a piano above his head.

Nathan squealed and bolted toward the jungle gym, glancing over his shoulder to see if his dad was following. "You can't catch me!" he hollered, scrambling onto a ladder as Sam gave chase.

"I'm getting closer!" Sam called, jogging after him. Nathan's giggles filled the air. When he reached the platform, Sam tackled him gently, wrapping him in a big hug. "Gotcha!" Sam said, tousling Nathan's hair. "You're mine now. I'm never letting you go."

Nathan squirmed and laughed. "Can we get something to eat?"

"Of course," Sam said, rising to his feet.

They wandered over to a line of food trucks at the park's edge. Burgers in hand, they settled beneath a grove of trees. Nathan nibbled at his food, pausing every so often to chase a bug or circle a tree, while Sam wolfed his down.

Spending time with his son acted as a balm for Sam's aching heart, but still couldn't repair it. Once or twice a week wasn't enough. Why should Jenny's ambivalence about their relationship interfere with his time with Nathan? He shoved the thought aside, unwilling to let it ruin the moment.

As the sun dipped lower in the sky, Nathan's yawns signaled the end of their outing. Sam packed up their trash, a wave of sadness crashing over him. Dropping Nathan off with Jenny meant missing out on bedtime snuggles and goodnight kisses. He hurled their trash into a nearby bin, the clang of metal echoing through the trees.

Nathan slipped his tiny, dirt-streaked hand into Sam's as they walked toward the car. Sam held it tightly, savoring the fleeting connection. After buckling Nathan into his seat, he climbed into the driver's side and headed to Jenny's house.

When they arrived, Sam knocked, and Jenny answered, her cellphone pressed to her ear. She mouthed, "Talking to my mom," as she took Nathan's hand. She smiled at their son but avoided meeting Sam's eyes.

"Thanks. Hope you had fun with him," she said over her shoulder, ushering Nathan inside. Before Sam could reply, the door closed firmly in his face.

Sam stood there for a moment, staring at the door. The thought of returning to his empty house, where his only companions were strangers on the other end of online video games, made his insides ache.

Chapter 16

A WEEK EARLIER, SAM had acquired a couch from a friend whose wife wanted a new sectional. Borrowing a minivan, he repeated the familiar ritual of moving into a new place: offering beer in exchange for muscle power to carry the sofa into his home.

The couch was well-used and far from pristine, but it gave him a place to relax besides his bed. Sprawling out, he tossed a few pillows behind his head, ignoring the faint odor of stale milk emanating from the cushions. The TV was on, but he wasn't paying attention. The video gamers had called it quits an hour ago, and he wasn't ready to fall asleep this early in the evening.

He pulled out his phone and texted Gina:

> You up for a chat? It's been a couple of days.

Her reply came almost instantly, making him smile.

> Sure. Maybe we can talk. Does now work for you?

Sam's heart raced as he typed back:

Now? Of course.

I'll call you in five minutes.

Unable to sit still, Sam bounced around the house to kill time. He made a pit stop in the bathroom, ensuring he wouldn't need to excuse himself mid-conversation. Glancing in the mirror, he debated whether Gina might suggest a video call. Probably not, he thought, but just in case, he made sure he didn't look too disheveled.

He returned to the couch and debated the best way to sit. Sprawling out felt too casual; he opted for a more upright posture. He rehearsed possible greetings aloud: "Hello, this is Sam Jordan," "Hi, Gina, so glad you had some time," and "Hellooooo." None felt right. Finally, he settled on warming up with a few scales to clear his throat and ensure his voice was strong.

After what felt like an eternity—seven minutes and forty-two seconds—his phone buzzed. He forced himself to wait a moment before answering, then casually said, "Hey."

"Hey, yourself," Gina responded, her voice light and warm.

Eager to avoid awkwardness, Sam replied, "I'm glad we could talk."

"Me too. I like the sound of your voice," she said.

"I hope this is a good time," he added.

"It is. My so-called husband just went back to work for some emergency. We argued earlier about how much he works, so your text was perfect timing," she giggled.

"I try. I can't believe you're the fighting type," he said, testing the waters.

"I don't think I am, but we seem to argue more lately. What about you?"

"Nah, I like to keep things simple. I'm a go-with-the-flow kind of guy." Sam deliberately avoided mentioning the state of his marriage; the less said, the better.

"That's always been your vibe," Gina said, her tone softening. "Maybe that's why I was drawn to you back then."

"What? "You were?"

"Of course. Don't tell me you didn't know. I still remember that kiss we shared by the lake. You were so into stargazing, teaching me all the constellations."

"But you never came back to the lake with me," Sam said, tinged with disbelief.

"Maybe not, but I wanted to. Sometimes you just feel a connection with someone. You were that person for me."

"Really?"

"Yeah. I've thought about it over the years. I wish we'd stayed in touch after camp. Who knows? Life might've turned out differently."

"What do you mean?" he asked, leaning forward.

"I don't know. Life is all about timing, isn't it? I met my husband not long after college. He's a solid guy, but sometimes I wonder—what if I'd met someone else at a different time? What if I'd met you when I was older? Maybe we'd have gotten to know each other better."

Sam hesitated, then said, "Well, we're older now."

"I know," she said. "That's why I was so happy to track you down—and find out you're nearby."

"It wouldn't be hard to meet up," Sam suggested, his heart pounding. "We could see each other."

"Oh, I'd love that. Would your wife mind?" she asked, her tone rising slightly.

"I don't think so. She's big on keeping in touch with old friends." And she kicked me out, so her opinion doesn't count, he thought bitterly.

"That's great. We could talk more about that lake kiss if we meet up."

"I'd like that," Sam said.

I'm so glad we connected," Gina said. "I have to get to work, but let's keep talking. I love hearing from you."

"I feel the same," Sam replied. "Can't wait to talk again."

After they disconnected, Sam sank back into the couch, grinning like an eighth grader. He replayed their conversation over and over in his head, the huskiness of her voice embedded in his brain, causing tingles to run up his spine.

Chapter 17

S AM MOVED ABOUT HIS apartment, tidying his socks and straightening the couch. Though dressed for work, he had little enthusiasm for going. His mind, preoccupied since his last call with Gina two days ago, swirled with vivid fantasies. She had become an obsession, dominating his thoughts by day and creeping into his dreams by night.

He picked up his phone and typed a text.

> **Time to chat?**

The reply came quickly:

> Pablo left an hour ago for work. I got a little time.

Sam had learned enough about her already to know this meant she wanted to talk, not chat. And whatever Gina wanted, Gina got. She didn't have to spell it out; he just knew.

After waiting what felt like an appropriate amount of time, he tapped on her contact in his phone. He'd saved her as "Henry Gottlieb," a playful nod to her initials—Hot Gina.

She answered on the first ring.

"Hey," she drawled, a sultry mix of warmth and Southern charm.

Sam couldn't help but feel captivated by how she made a single word sound irresistible. He wanted more.

"I think we should have dinner," he blurted out.

She laughed. "Well, I think we should too. It's a spectacular idea."

His heart raced. Taking a deep breath, he moved the phone away to avoid revealing his excitement. "I can drive up to meet you. How's this weekend?"

"You move fast. I like that. Saturday works. Pablo has plans in the evening, as usual. There's a cozy little restaurant close to here. Would you want to go there?"

"Of course. Sounds perfect." He paused, then added with a smirk, "Should we invite Trevor Morrison?"

Her laugh deepened, hearty and full of amusement. "No, that's not a great idea. He wasn't much for talking—lots of grunting, though. Not exactly a stellar conversationalist. Besides, last I heard, he's somewhere in California. A bit far for dinner. Bummer."

Sam could picture her exaggerated pout. So damn cute. "Probably for the best," he said. "I never liked him much anyway."

"Ah, the things we do when we're young. Everything would be different if I knew then what I know now."

How would anything be different? he wondered. "He wasn't much of a guitarist either," Sam said, wanting to tease her a bit.

"I know! You don't even know how many times I had to sit through his 'performances.' So dreadful."

They laughed together, a shared moment of levity. Sam marveled at how easily she dismissed Trevor Morrison while simultaneously agreeing to dinner with him. For the first time in weeks, a flicker of confidence surged through him.

They talked a while longer before Gina reluctantly excused herself, claiming work called. Before hanging up, she promised to send him the restaurant details.

Sam sat back, head swimming with anticipation. He pictured the two of them at dinner, her laughter floating across the table. Then he fantasized about her inviting him somewhere afterward where they would be alone, her leaning in, eyes locking with his as she whispered, "I love you, Sam Jordan."

Chapter 18

THE DAY OF HIS dinner with Gina dragged from the start. Sitting alone for hours made time feel frozen. After cycling through outfit after outfit, Sam finally settled on a gray pair of pants and a striped chenille shirt Jenny had bought him shortly before she kicked him out of the house. He agonized over whether to buy her flowers or bring a gift, but ultimately decided against it. He didn't want it to seem like he thought this was a date--even though, deep down, that was exactly what he hoped it would be.

Playing it cool was crucial. No mentions of the attention he craved from her back at camp. No hints of how often he thought about her since. She couldn't know how much this meeting meant to him.

During the two-hour drive up the turnpike, he rehearsed lines to throw out and stories from his past to tell to avoid any awkward silences. He wanted to impress her, but it had to seem effortless. It had been years since he'd been gone out with anyone other than Jenny, and even though this wasn't supposed to be a date, his clammy hands and cracking voice betrayed his nerves as he muttered to himself.

He drove north toward her semi-rural town—a place of open farmland and large lots where neighbors were hidden from view. Off the turnpike, winding roads led him to the restaurant Gina had chosen.

The Oakley was tucked back on its property, surrounded by birch and oak trees. A gravel path led from the parking lot to its entrance, understated under a simple sign. He chuckled when he noticed the building was attached to a rustic inn, its dark wood exterior hinting at cozy, intimate accommodations.

The setting felt perfect--secluded, unpretentious, with a touch of class. He took it as a good sign that she had chosen this as their meeting spot.

Inside the Oakley's dimly lit lobby, Sam's eyes took a moment to adjust. Small, candlelit tables lined the walls—this wasn't a place for noisy family gatherings. It was a haven for couples seeking privacy, where quiet conversation, not partying, would flourish.

Sam ran his fingers through his hair as he checked his reflection in a mirror hanging on the wall. He was satisfied with his look, but his heart raced as a wave of dizziness passed through him. He forced a deep breath.

A tap on his arm startled him, jerking him back to the present. Gina stood before him, smiling, her black strapless dress hugging her curves. Her legs seemed endless beneath its high hemline, and a slim black purse, almost invisible, hung over her shoulder. Sam forced himself to meet her gaze, captivated by how her mascara made her dark eyes stand out.

He hesitated but stepped toward her. She wrapped him in a warm hug. "I'm so glad to see you. Thanks for driving all this way," she whispered, her breath tickling his ear and sending chills down his back.

The hostess, dressed in an outfit similar to Gina's, but less daring, led them to a booth. As Gina walked ahead, her hips swayed just enough to capture Sam's attention. He forced his focus onto the path ahead, trying to steady his thoughts.

Once seated, the flickering candlelight cast a soft glow between them. Gina reached across the table, placing her hand on his. "I'm so excited. It's been ages." She giggled, withdrawing her hand. "Start dishing—we've got so much to catch up on." Her smile revealed gleaming, perfect teeth.

Sam returned her smile but couldn't figure out what to do with his hands. After a brief internal struggle, he clasped them under the table to keep them still. "You want a drink?" he blurted, congratulating himself for sounding normal.

She nodded. "Yes, definitely. I'm a little nervous—it'll help." Her hand brushed his again before pulling back.

He flagged the server, who promptly took their orders.

He glanced at his menu, but then put it aside. "So, it's been fifteen years since I've seen you," he said. "You look even better than you did back at camp."

She lowered her gaze before meeting his eyes again. "You always said the sweetest things. I've wondered about you so often over the years."

He shifted in his seat. "I've thought about you, too. A lot. I've wondered how life's treated you since camp."

She waved a dismissive hand. "We've texted plenty about that. Let's talk about now."

Before he could respond, the server arrived to take their food order. They also asked for another round of drinks.

As Gina spoke, Sam couldn't help but sneak glances at her. Time had only enhanced her allure. Her once-cute features were now strikingly refined, her expertly styled hair cascading to her shoulders. She was still whip-smart, but now she owned it unapologetically. Sam felt both intimidated and determined to hold her interest.

By their second round of Cosmos, he began to spill some of his inner thoughts and express his ambivalence about his life. "My wife kicked me out two months ago. I'm in this crummy townhouse now."

Gina's sympathetic expression and the gentle touch of her hand on his reinforced his desire to open up to her. "I'm so sorry," she said softly. "Things aren't great in my marriage, either." She hesitated, then added, "Maybe we can figure this out together."

Sam wasn't looking for pity. He didn't want to dwell on Jenny or Gina's husband. He shook his head slightly, trying to clear his thoughts.

"I'm just. . . figuring things out as I go," he said. "I'm open to whatever's next."

"I get that." Her voice wavered. "Some nights, I lie in bed crying while he sleeps beside me, oblivious."

Sam's brow furrowed. "How could he not notice?" He leaned forward.

She shrugged. "He's always working, always gone. Truthfully, I'm bored." She paused. "But I still want to make it work."

Sam felt a flicker of hope. Was she leaving the door open for him? He didn't want to misstep, so he changed the subject, steering the conversation toward lighter topics—old friends, work, camp memories, and a brief reminiscence of Trevor Morrison. Talking to her was easy, the conversation flowed without effort. Her laughter filled the space between them, and for the first time in weeks, Sam felt truly at ease.

Talking with her was easy. Conversation flowed so smoothly he thought they started to complete each other's sentences. He hadn't laughed so much in weeks and loved whenever she cracked up at what he was saying.

When the plates were cleared, Gina declined dessert. "I'd bust out of this dress," she joked, patting her stomach.

He smiled and began to reach for his wallet. She lifted a finger. "How about one more drink?"

Sam's smile widened. "Absolutely." He motioned to the server, who in less than a minute returned with their order.

"To old friends," Sam toasted.

"To getting to know old friends better," she said in a whisper. He tilted his glass forward for them to clink together, and with perhaps a little excess gusto, she extended her arm forward, smashing her glass into his. His glass shattered, causing a waterfall, most of which landed on him.

She looked horrified at the mess and then at Sam's face where liquid dripped down his cheeks. "Oh no. I'm so sorry. I'm such a klutz." She glanced at his hand which had trickles of blood near his thumb. "I cut you. Are you okay?"

He laughed. "You can't hurt me. It's only a flesh wound."

She reached behind to the empty adjoining booth and grabbed a folded, white napkin. She dabbed it on his hand and soon tiny droplets of red dotted the cloth. "I've made a mess of you." She continued to press the linen against his hand while using her other to support it underneath. She pulled his hand closer and kissed his wrist. "I think you need to rinse it under water."

Sam nodded. "I'll run to the restroom. This will be quick."

"I'm so sorry," she called out, as he left the table.

Less than five minutes later, he returned looking like nothing had happened. He held up his hand to show her there were no open cuts, just a few pin pricks of red.

"I'm so awkward sometimes," she said, shaking her head.

"Don't think about it. Kind of funny, actually." He looked at her and put his hand on top of hers. "I had an amazing time tonight. Do you think we can do it again?"

She turned her hand over, so their palms were together. "I loved this. I only wish we had done it sooner. You're such a great guy." She glanced at the time on her phone. "I need to get home," she said, sticking out her lower lip.

He walked her to her car thinking about how the evening might end. He wanted to kiss her, and hold her, and take her clothes off. What did she want?

When they reached where she had parked, she turned to him. "I want to see you again. Really soon." She leaned into him and engulfed him in a full hug, caressing the nape of neck. He rubbed her back and wanted to let his hands wander lower. She pressed in further, and then released, letting out a huge breath of air.

"Thanks, baby," she said. "Such a great evening." She smiled and let herself into her car. As she drove out of the parking lot, he rubbed his hands through his hair. It would be a long, lonely ride home. But for the first time in a while, he felt a spark of something more.

Chapter 19

THE ROAD STRETCHED AHEAD, dark and empty except for the occasional passing headlights. Sam set the cruise control, leaned back in his seat, and let his thoughts drift to the evening. His first impression--she was still stunning. Absolutely gorgeous. But there was more—so much more. She was funny, smart, and articulate. He couldn't think of a single thing about her that didn't draw him in. Her laugh lingered in his mind, and her scent teased his imagination. Other than her superhuman strength while making a toast, she seemed flawless.

Then, reality hit. She was married.

Still, she'd emphasized how unhappy she was. He couldn't recall her exact words, but it was clear she felt trapped. And she'd kept touching him. That had to mean something, right?

As he drove, questions circled like a cyclone. Was he misreading the signs? Was this a repeat of their summer camp years? Did she still see him as just a good friend?

Too many questions. Not enough answers.

He tapped the screen on his dashboard and called Gregg. His friend answered after one ring, his gravelly voice filled with curiosity.

"Hey, how'd your evening go with the queen of the ball?"

"Shut up. You know she's not like that."

"Of course." Gregg's sarcasm was thick. "So, what happened?"

"It was. . . amazing. So easy."

For the next fifteen minutes, Sam recounted the dinner, leaning heavily on the laughter and the way she'd touched his arm—again and again. Gregg listened with minimal interruptions, throwing in the occasional "Interesting," or "No way!"

When Sam finally described the goodbye at her car, Gregg spoke up. "Sounds like it went just like you wanted it to. So, what's next?"

"I have no idea. Don't know if it's my move or hers."

"Tough call."

Sam was about to offer his own theory when a ringing sound came through his speakers. The display flashed: Henry Gottlieb Calling.

He struggled to keep his eyes on the road. "Holy crap. It's her!"

"Tell her I said, 'Hi,'" Gregg said with a chuckle.

Sam ended the call and picked up the incoming one. "Hey, couldn't wait until I got home?"

There was no laughter in response. Instead, her voice quivered with anger. "I'm so upset. Pablo's not here. He left me a message saying he's working late and told me not to wait up." She was pissed.

Sam frowned. "Did he know when you'd be home?"

"Yes." She drew the word out, her frustration clear. "He knew. He's always playing these stupid games. I think he's seeing someone else."

"Are you sure?"

"There've been signs. A woman knows these things." Her voice tightened. "I'm so angry. You'd never do something like that, would you?"

"I never have." Sam paused. "Would you?"

"I don't know anymore. Tonight's got me thinking. You were so sweet and funny. Pablo says the right things, but he doesn't mean them. His actions never match his words." She pushed out a rush of air. "He doesn't understand me the way you do."

Sam hesitated. "Why do you think I understand you so well?"

"I can just tell. You understood me back then, and I was too stupid to see it. I thought Trevor Morrison was the coolest, but I ignored you."

Sam's grip on the steering wheel tightened. "Keep going."

"Pablo's just like Trevor. Checks all the boxes—good looks, lots of money—but what does it matter if he doesn't treat me right?"

"Not much," Sam said, hoping she would continue to spew.

"You're so right. You've always been. I realized so much tonight. I need to make changes. Real changes."

"What are you looking to do?"

"I need to figure out how to be done with Pablo."

Sam's pulse quickened. "You mean divorce?"

She hesitated. "I can't. He made me sign all these documents when we got married. 'Just in case,' he said. If I leave, I'll have nothing. I'm not starting over."

"So. . . what are you saying?"

"I think you know."

"I don't," Sam insisted.

"When we were at dinner, I wanted you to grab me and kiss me. In the parking lot, it took everything not to throw myself at you. I know you felt it too."

His throat tightened. This was what he'd wanted for years. "Of course. You know how I feel." His voice quivered, and he had to make sure he was concentrating on the road. His mind was everywhere.

"I've known, baby. I just needed to hear it."

Sam's thoughts spun. "What do we do?"

"I don't know. I haven't figured it all out yet."

"Well, we've got time. We need to get together again. See where this goes."

"Definitely. I want it fun and easy, like tonight. No strings attached."

"I'm all in."

"Good. Next time, don't leave me standing in the parking lot."

"I won't."

He hoped the conversation would continue, but her tone abruptly changed.

"Shit. Pablo's coming up the driveway. I've got to go. Let's talk soon. Can we meet for dinner again?"

"Of course," Sam began to say, but the line went dead.

He stared at the empty road ahead, her voice still echoing in his mind. She wanted him—had always wanted him. Why hadn't she said so before? What was holding her back now?

The questions came fast and furious, but as he approached his exit, he realized he was once again left with no answers.

Chapter 20

THROUGH THE KITCHEN WINDOW, Sam watched Jenny walk up the path to his townhouse. He'd recently placed a few flowerpots out front to make the place a bit more inviting and felt a flicker of satisfaction when she stooped to smell the geraniums. It wasn't a palace, but since moving in, he'd made it homier, which in no small measure, disheartened him as it reflected the reality of the looming permanence of his new living situation.

Her shorts flattered her legs without being obvious about it, and her t-shirt did the same for the rest of her figure. With her hair tied back, she still had that girl-next-door charm, a bittersweet reminder that she was no longer the woman he shared his life with.

His friends had always said she was out of his league. Her success at nearly everything contrasted sharply with his perpetual sputtering through life, leaving him with little reason to argue their assessment. In the end, it was she who pulled away—not completely, but enough. She still visited, dropping vague hints about a future where they might be together again.

As Jenny neared the front door, Sam found himself comparing her to Gina. Jenny could still turn heads, but she didn't exude

Gina's unapologetic confidence. Gina, with her curve-hugging attire and bold demeanor, seemed to revel in the attention she commanded. It was the old Ginger versus Mary Ann debate—or maybe Jennifer Marlowe versus Bailey Quarters. These relics from TV history flickered through his mind, and he smirked, chiding himself for spending too much time watching reruns.

"It's hot out there," Jenny said, brushing a bead of sweat from her forehead as she stepped inside.

Sam offered her a glass of water, which she accepted. He led her to the kitchen, where she dropped into one of the chairs around a modest table. "These are comfy," she said, running her hand along the backrest. "Were they here last time?"

"I've gotten a lot of new stuff," he said, gesturing around the room. "Looks like I'm not leaving anytime soon."

Jenny pouted, but her voice rang with hope. "I still need more time."

Sam's expression darkened. "That's crap," he said, his brow creasing. "You always need more time. I've given you months. You're just stalling."

Her face softened as she reached out, but he pulled his hand away. "I'm not stalling, Sam. I'm trying to figure out what I want."

"You've had more than enough time," he shot back. "I'm starting to figure things out for myself."

Jenny tilted her head. "Like what?"

"Like the fact that you don't get to make all the decisions. I have a say in what happens too." He stood abruptly, pacing to the other side of the kitchen with his back turned to her.

Jenny rolled her eyes. "What have you decided?" she asked, her voice measured but edged with irritation.

"I don't like the way you've treated me," he said, turning to face her. "And it's not like I don't have options."

She raised an eyebrow. "What are you talking about?"

"I'm not just sitting around waiting for you to decide. I've got options, Jenny."

"Like what?" she pressed, sounding skeptical.

"Just like you and Bill Harkins," he said, his volume rising. "I can go out too."

Her eyes narrowed. "Bill Harkins? I told you, there's nothing there. He's just a friend."

"But you went out with him, didn't you?"

"So what?"

"So, I'm doing the same thing."

Jenny leaned back in her chair, crossing her arms. "Who are you going out with?"

"I don't have to tell you," Sam said with a shrug. "But we had a great time."

"Oh."

Sam didn't intend to hurt Jenny, but a small part of him relished the sting in her reaction. He looked around his new home, a surge of injustice rising in his chest. No one deserved to be pushed out of their life or separated from their kid. What right did she have to do this to him? He had been a supportive husband and a good father. His simmering grievances boiled over, eclipsing any effort at restraint.

He moved closer, looming over her. "I'm not going to sit around waiting anymore. I've got to look out for myself."

Jenny bit her lip, saying nothing.

"And you're not perfect either," Sam continued, his voice still rising. "You're always quick to point out my faults, but let's talk about yours. You don't like to cook, so I do it all. You think your sarcasm is funny, but it's not. It's hurtful. You tear me apart every chance you get."

A single tear slid down Jenny's cheek. She pushed her chair back and stood. "Pick Nate up tomorrow afternoon—whatever time works for you. I'll have everything ready. Just bring him back before bedtime." She headed for the door, pausing with her hand on the handle. "I hope that wasn't too hurtful for you." Without a glance back, she stepped outside.

Sam watched from the window as she walked down the path, wiping her eyes. He stood frozen, wondering how he managed to screw everything up in such a short period.

Chapter 21

MAKING JENNY CRY LEFT Sam in a lurch. The mixture of a dose of superiority combined with a dash of regret churned in the pit of his stomach as he replayed their latest interaction, berating himself for how poorly he had handled it.

She had been the one who dumped him forcing him to move out while dangling just enough hope she would take him back. He didn't deserve her condescension. She'd never acknowledged the sacrifices he had made—taking a back seat as her career flourished by managing the house and caring for Nate—all of which provided her the freedom to nurture her friendships and thrive professionally.

Lashing out at her hadn't been part of his plan. It just happened, a natural response to the situation she had put him in, a reflex born of frustration and hurt. But the more he thought about it, the more he rationalized: she had created this situation. If she felt a little pain as a result, maybe she should look in the mirror?

Even as he perseverated on his encounter with Jenny, his mind wandered to Gina. Unlike Jenny, Gina hadn't belittled him. She heap attention on him—validated him. The dinner they'd shared kept replaying in his head, especially the way she'd stroked his ego.

He had texted her after their dinner, eager to talk more, but her responses had been distant. She wasn't as open as she'd been when they had chatted on his way home.

Frustration mounting, Sam picked up his phone to text her again.

My wife just left. Big fight. Can you talk?

Not really.

Just looking for advice. She doesn't get me sometimes. I'm not sure what to do about it. Any advice?

Not really. What do you think?

I need to give this more thought. Maybe time will help me figure this out.

Sounds like a plan. Hope it works out for you. I think you're on your way.

Maybe we can get together to discuss?

Not right now. I need space. Pablo and I are trying to prioritize time together. I'm pretty booked.

Really? There's so much to talk about.

> Sure. I enjoyed seeing you, but we'll catch up again eventually.

When?

> Who knows? Like I said, Pablo and I are focusing on us.

That's different than what you said before.

> I hope not. Like I told you, we're looking to start a family. We need this time.

Can't we have dinner again?

> Not right now. Let me get back to you. Pablo and I are heading out now. Take care.

And just like that, the conversation was over. No matter how long he stared at his phone and offered prayers to a god he hadn't spoken to for a while, no more messages came. Despair settled over him like a weight, paralyzing him. His stomach churned as he leaned back on the couch. His entire body ached. What had changed? The Gina he had laughed with over drinks seemed like a distant memory.

The prospect of spending time with her had consumed him, and now there was a void where that hope had been. He thought about Jenny and how he'd hurt her. In less than an hour, his relationships with the two most important women in his life had been damaged seemingly beyond repair.

His pulse raced. He pressed a hand to his chest. A panic attack loomed.

Then his phone rang, startling him out of his stupor. He grabbed it and kissed it when he saw it was Gina. He sat up straight and took a deep, long gulp of air before answering with what he hoped was a casual tone. "Hey, I thought you didn't want to talk to me anymore."

He heard her sniffling, her breath unsteady. Concern overtook his initial excitement. "Are you okay?"

"I'm fine," she said, though her voice betrayed her. "Just been crying. Give me a minute to collect my thoughts."

"Take your time. I'm here."

She took a deep cleansing breath before continuing. "I'm sorry about those texts. Pablo walked in while I was messaging you. I panicked. I didn't want him to see what I was typing."

Sam's heart pounded. "Are you okay? Are you in danger?"

"I don't think so," she said with a heavy sigh. "I've just been so confused since our dinner. Seeing you stirred up a lot of feelings."

"It sounded like you wanted to patch things up with him."

"I'm so sorry. Like I said, I panicked. I do want to see you again—but we have to be careful."

"You know I want to see you. Let me know when and where."

There was a pause before she asked, "Can you meet next Friday? Same restaurant. Can you make a reservation? I'll meet you there like before."

"Of course. Whatever you want."

Her voice dropped to a whisper. "Maybe... maybe you can book a hotel room there too?"

Sam's breath caught. "Absolutely. Great idea."

She giggled softly. "I think it's best if we don't communicate until then. Pablo might be checking my phone.

"Smart," he agreed, though the thought of silence bothered him. "I can't wait. It'll be hard not hearing from you, but it'll be worth it."

"It will be," she said, full of hope. "I'll make it worth it. I promise."

They ended the call with affirmations of enthusiasm and anticipation. Sam wanted to declare his love, to ask her to leave everything for him, but he held back. Yet, the few minutes speaking with Gina had pushed away his shame about how he had treated Jenny.

As soon as they hung up, he made the reservations—a table at the Oakley and a hotel room complete with champagne on ice. His imagination ran wild, and he made no effort to reign it in.

For the first time that evening, he felt at peace, no longer burdened by guilt over Jenny.

Chapter 22

THE DRIVE TO DINNER felt endless. Sam struggled to contain his excitement, his eyes darting to the GPS every few minutes, as though he could will the distance to shrink. For a moment, the beauty of the tree-lined highway distracted him, the tall pines standing like silent sentinels in the fading sunlight. But soon, his thoughts drifted back to Gina and the promise of the evening ahead.

He reminded himself to stay grounded, to let the night unfold naturally rather than rushing ahead. Still, the image of the hotel room flickered in his thoughts. That would be where he'd finally tell her everything he'd been holding back since they met at camp, and what her reintroduction into his life meant to him. The idea of being alone with her made his pulse quicken.

He imagined her in a slinky, low-cut top, her laughter filling the room as she leaned in close. He pictured himself sliding it off her shoulders, his hands trembling at the thought. Sweat slicked his palms, and his heart pounded against his ribs. Just a few more hours until I touch her, until her lips find mine, he thought. The intensity of his feelings overwhelmed his ability to focus on driving, so he forced himself to calm down by naming the lineup of the 1979 Pirates aloud, a trick he'd learned to distract himself when waiting for a jury verdict.

With the car windows down, and the wind blowing through his hair, he cranked up the music, drumming the steering wheel with nervous energy. When he finally reached his turnoff, he followed the narrow, stone road past the Pine Ridge Lodge. A smirk crossed his face as he pulled into the restaurant's gravel parking lot.

After smoothing his hair and grabbing the blazer draped over the backseat, he retrieved the bouquet of flowers he'd selected earlier in the day--a half dozen lilies with a single red rose in the middle. "This is going to be a night we talk about for years," he murmured to himself. "I'm going to savor every moment."

Inside, he checked in at the front desk, greeted warmly as though he were a regular. He had intended to wait for Gina by the bar, but the hostess reassured him that she'd escort her to their table the moment she arrived. Reluctantly, he followed her to a quiet corner of the restaurant and took a seat.

When the server stopped by, Sam ordered a vodka tonic. He planned to switch to something more celebratory when Gina arrived, but for now, he needed something to settle his nerves. He tapped his fingers on the table, glancing around the room, trying not to look as jittery as he felt.

Since graduating college, he'd developed a disdain for dining alone. To him, solo diners always looked lonely, even desperate. He preferred the bustle of a group, the camaraderie of shared meals. Sitting by himself now made him uncomfortably self-conscious.

He imagined the other diners casting judgmental glances his way, though they seemed more absorbed in their own meals.

He drained his drink and signaled for another. As each new arrival walked through the restaurant's entrance, his hope swelled—only to deflate when it wasn't Gina. With every passing minute, anxiety coiled tighter in his chest. He fiddled with the sugar packets on the table, folded and refolded his napkin, and watched the minutes on the clock on his phone tick by.

An hour passed. Still no Gina. A siren wailed in the distance, snapping him from his trance. It reminded him to check his messages again. His heart sank when he found nothing: no text, no voicemail, no missed call.

Unable to suppress his growing unease, he typed out a message:

> Hey, I'm waiting at the restaurant. Let me know when you're on your way.

Minutes crawled by with no response. He typed again:

> Still here. Where are you?

He stared at his phone, willing it to light up with a reply, but the silence mocked him. Twenty more minutes passed before he could admit the truth to himself: she wasn't coming. A wave of humiliation and disappointment washed over him, heavy and unrelenting.

When the server returned, he asked for the check. He tried to keep his composure, but the sting of rejection burned deep. No Gina. No wild night. No bliss.

As he pocketed his phone, a flicker of hope urged him to try one last time. Against his better judgment, he sent another message:

> I'm leaving. Let me know if everything's okay, if you can.

He shoved his phone in his pocket and walked out of the restaurant unable to make eye contact with anyone. He tossed the flowers in the trash.

Chapter 23

O UT OF UNSHAKABLE OPTIMISM, or perhaps a sign of his unwavering faith in Gina, Sam drove down the short drive to the Inn. It was now a renovated Mediterranean-style hotel, built one hundred and fifty years earlier, with understated elegance accentuated by the soft glow of accent lighting along its base.

He stepped into the small lobby, crossing the vast Persian rug that stretched across the stone floor. Two petite leather couches faced one another off to the side, a long oak table between them. The lighting was dim, supplemented by a cylindrical metal candelabra with a ring of flickering candles.

As Sam neared the front desk, he offered a quick prayer that Gina might surprise him in their room. A young man, dressed stylishly with cropped, dyed blonde hair, greeted him. His name tag read, "Caspar." "Hi. I'm Sam Jordan. I have a reservation for tonight. I wanted to check if anyone might have already checked into my room."

The man shot Sam a confused look. "Is the room under your name?"

Sam nodded.

"We wouldn't allow anyone else to check into your room unless you'd already arrived. But let me double-check," he said, scrolling through his computer before shaking his head. "Nothing. Would you like to check in?"

"I was hoping to cancel the room. I won't need it."

The young man clicked his tongue while rolling his eyes. "I'm sorry, sir. You've prepaid for the room. Unfortunately, we cannot cancel it."

Sam wasn't surprised. "Nothing's going right. I guess I should check-in and take the room after all."

"My pleasure." The man typed on his computer and then printed a key card, handing it across the counter.

An overwhelming sense of emptiness washed over Sam as he opened the door to what should have been their room. A plush king-sized bed with soft linens and satiny pillows sat at the far end. A cozy seating area with two armchairs nestled into the corner.

Elegant artwork adorned the walls, and tasteful knickknacks rested on the horizontal surfaces. To his right, a spacious bathroom with a soaking tub and a rain shower beckoned. Soft, fluffy towels were neatly stacked on the shelves. He imagined Gina in the comfy bathrobe hanging on the door.

As he stepped farther into the room, he noticed a bottle of champagne chilling in a bucket of ice, with two flutes poised beside it. Chocolate-covered strawberries rested on a bone-white plate, with a dish of whipped cream beside them. The hotel had followed his instructions to the letter.

He grabbed the bottle by its neck, pausing to imagine making a toast with Gina. Something like, "Hoping we get to know each other better as adults," followed by her laughter and a sip, her eyes locked on his.

With a surge of anger tearing through him, he ripped the bottle from the ice bucket and twisted off the cork. Champagne sprayed everywhere, soaking the bed and dripping onto the floor. His anger was augmented by an overwhelming wave of frustration sweeping over him. Why didn't he ever get what he wanted? What he deserved? Life just wasn't fair.

He took a long gulp of champagne, and without thinking, hurled the bottle against the wall. It shattered, sending a spray of glass across the room. Sam looked at the mess, shrugged, and walked out.

Chapter 24

THE DRIBBLES OF SUNLIGHT pushed a bit of light into Sam's place, but his mood remained dark. He paced from the dining area into the kitchen on a loop, just as he had been doing for the past twenty minutes. The entire day, his thoughts had fixated on Gina, trying to figure out why she'd blown him off for dinner. Ignoring the work he should have been doing, he kept staring at his phone, hoping for any message from her. It never came, despite sending a couple of brief texts hours ago.

He was at a loss for what to do. Jenny still wouldn't talk to him, only sending a message outlining when he should pick up and drop off Nate. The concept of doing normal errands or managing family relationships felt foreign to him, his mind consumed by Gina's failure to make contact.

His game console sat on the ground near the television, tossed in anger when he returned from his disappointing non-encounter the night before. The idea of playing was so unappealing, as he knew it wouldn't distract him from the constant thoughts of Gina. Yet, with nothing else to do, he logged on, hoping somehow it might alter his mood.

With his headset on and the game loading, he flopped back onto the couch. Three of the guys he often teamed with were already online, so he joined them. The killing of enemy teams started immediately, but Sam found little joy in it, even as they wiped out the competition. His lifetime statistics, scrolling across the screen after each battle, improved with the victory. His satisfaction with his life, however, dropped to an all-time low.

While they waited for the next contest, Sam tried to engage his teammates through his headset.

"Hey guys, how's everyone doing?"

No response.

"Anybody got anything they want to share?"

Silence.

"I'm feeling like crap."

Still nothing.

"I've had a rough time. Anybody want to know what's happening to me?"

Dead silence.

He was about to ask another question but noticed that two of his teammates had logged off. No point in burdening the last one with more attempts at connecting on a personal level. Maybe it was a little too intimate for a bunch of fifteen-year-olds.

Sam threw his controller to the side. Playing had done nothing to reduce his anxiety. At least he'd killed fifteen minutes without too much obsessing over Gina. Now, he faced another restless night of sleep, his mind spinning with incessant questions about why she had blown him off.

Not quite ready for bed and unable to concentrate on reading or anything else, he decided to check Facebook to see if Gina had posted anything. She wasn't a prolific poster, and Sam rarely spent much time scrolling through her feed, but what he saw shook him to his core.

An hour earlier, she had posted:

"I need your prayers. Last night, while I was out, my wonderful husband Pablo was murdered in our home. Needless to say, I'm out of my mind, but I wanted everyone to hear it from me before the news spreads. Will you, my dear friends, please pray for his soul? I'm devastated but wanted all of you to know. I remain hopeful that during this time of tragedy, you can respect my desire for privacy. I love all of you dearly."

Below the post, she shared a picture of her and Pablo, smiling as they held hands.

Sam almost fell out of his chair. It felt like a gut punch—like he was grieving the loss himself. Her husband had been the victim of a random act of violence. It was heartbreaking.

He scrolled down, reading the hundreds of comments beneath her post. They started as sympathy and support but soon devolved into speculation, with people guessing at what had happened. No one had any real answers—just wild theories.

Sam googled "Pablo Marcon," and found a couple of small articles that had been published in the past few hours. The first, from a tiny news outlet in Gina's area, read:

"Last evening, respected businessman Pablo Marcon was found murdered in his bedroom from two gunshot wounds. Local police are investigating the murder. There were no signs of forced entry, but a botched robbery is suspected. The victim's wife, Gina Marcon, a nurse at Provident General, returned home from shopping to find her husband. Authorities have not identified any suspects."

Sam searched through the crevices of the internet, but couldn't find any additional details. As much as his heart went out to Gina for her loss, his anxiety began to subside. There could be no better reason for her to have blown him off than the tragic death of her husband. He understood now why she hadn't shown up—she was dealing with something far more significant. Trying to process it all, he realized that maybe she hadn't blown him off at all.

He dashed off a text to her:

> I just found out what happened to Pablo. I'm so sorry for your loss. I hope you're okay, and I'm thinking of you.

He put his phone down, praying that his words would offer her some small measure of comfort in her time of loss.

Chapter 25

THE WORK WAS PILED high on his desk, waiting for Sam to attack it. Depositions for review were to his right, discovery requests to be drafted to his left, and his computer, with at least thirty emails needing responses, stared back at him. Yet, for the past forty minutes, the paralysis of mind and body had kept him from doing anything.

He had dragged himself into the office, but his mind still fixated on Gina. He wanted to be supportive, but had no idea what she needed or how to offer support. His chair creaked as he leaned back, pondering his next move, until sudden clarity hit him.

The funeral. In that moment, his next step was clear.

I'll go, pay my respects, and get a better sense of the situation. She'll think I'm considerate, and it could set the stage for when she's done grieving.

The thought of taking action made his heart rate slow, and for the first time since she hadn't shown, his breathing felt less labored. He bit his lower lip and pulled up Facebook to see if there were any updates on the burial. One of her friends had commented on Gina's last post, saying the service would be held at Gina and

Pablo's church in three days. He marked the funeral on his calendar, then turned back to the stacks on his desk. But once again, focus eluded him.

Against his better judgment, he picked up his phone. His heart skipped a beat when a notification appeared—Gina had texted him. Finally, he thought, she's going to explain everything.

He tapped the screen with trembling fingers. Blood drained from his face as he read:

> I'm not sure why you're trying to contact me. Please stop. Never contact me again. I don't want to hear from you.

That was it? What the hell was that?

In the time it took to read her message, Sam's world once again spiraled into chaos. He buried his face in his hands and began banging his head against the desk. He would've kept going for the next hour, but a knock on the door interrupted his self-punishment.

"Yes?" he said, lifting his head and forcing a smile, trying not to let his emotions rule his facial expressions. "Come in."

Gary Gerber poked his head in. "Got a minute?"

Not really, Sam thought, not wanting to talk to anyone. Despite liking Gerber, he had no desire to endure another conversation with him, especially not while staring at the same green sports coat Gerber wore three days a week. Sam's mind wasn't ready to listen to anyone, but Gerber was the boss.

Gerber entered and walked over to the window, his back to Sam. He fiddled with the blinds, silent for a moment. The smell of stale cigars clung to his coat, making Sam resort to mouth-breathing, waiting for Gerber to speak.

Finally, Gerber broke the silence. "How's everything?"

Sam's mind raced. Seriously? Everything sucks. My wife left me, this other woman won't talk to me, and now you're here to offer advice?

Instead, he said, "Amazing. How've you been?"

Gerber didn't catch the irony. "Everything's dandy. Evelyn and I are going to dinner tonight. We're driving to the shore this weekend."

"Sounds amazing." Sam rolled his eyes, a wave of dread about getting older washed over him.

Gerber sat down in the chair across from the desk. "I wanted to talk about your workload. We're concerned that not enough new files are coming in."

"So far, I'm good. I've got a few briefs to write, and I'm scheduled for depositions in two cases, which should fill my next two weeks."

"Good, because Mick and I were thinking we want you to take on more of the marketing effort, so we can keep a steady stream of business. We're trying to make you familiar with all aspects of the business. We hope to make you partner soon."

Sam nodded. He'd heard this pitch before—dangle the part-nership, make him bill more hours. It wasn't that he didn't have free time to market the firm, but the idea of taking clients out to dinner or schmoozing them over drinks made his skin crawl.

"Sure. Whatever's necessary." It was the same conversation they'd had a month ago, and the same one they'd have in a few weeks. So far, nothing had changed, so he wasn't worried.

Gerber turned toward the door. Sam silently offered thanks as the conversation seemed to be winding down. But before Gerber could grab the handle, the door flew open, and Randi, their newest secretary, rushed in, out of breath, her hair di-sheveled. She had run up the stairs—something Sam couldn't remember anyone ever doing before.

"The police," she coughed out. "They're downstairs. They have a warrant. For you."

She bent over, trying to catch her breath, and pointed to-ward Sam. He looked behind himself as though there might be someone else in the room, then swiveled back around with a "who me?' look on his face.

Randi nodded and pointed toward the stairs. "They said, 'Immediately, or they'll come up and drag you out.'"

Gerber sized Sam up and down, like his clothes were dirty. "I suspect you'd better get your ass down there."

Sam dashed around his desk, grabbed his suit jacket from the hook behind the door, and took the stairs two at a time.

At the bottom, he froze. Three uniformed officers stood shoulder-to-shoulder. All were well over six feet tall and none looked like they'd come for a casual chat.

The most sizable one, standing in the center, stepped forward. "Are you Samuel C. Jordan?" His voice was gruff and authoritative.

Sam nodded. "I am." His voice quivered slightly, so he cleared his throat.

"I'm Officer Giolitto from Elk County. We have a warrant for your arrest. You are hereby charged with the murder of Pablo Marcon."

Sam stood dumbfounded. "Who the hell is Pablo Marcon?" he shouted, then it hit him. Pablo Marcon. Gina's husband.

The circumstances swirling about his life—his wife leaving, his career tanking, Gina disappearing, and now a phalanx of police at his work with a warrant for his arrest—all coalesced at once in one overwhelming wave, making him nauseous. Without any conscious thought, he extended his hands, and as one of the officers reached for his handcuffs, he turned his head and heaved all over the area rug by the reception desk.

As the officers escorted Sam out, Gerber pointed at the vomit on the floor. "Well, looks like the stain of his existence at this firm will outlast his actual presence. Never seen anyone leave quite like this."

Chapter 26

T HEY SAY YOU GET one call when you're thrown in jail, and to Sam's dismay, the urban myth appeared to be true. The phone was an old-fashioned, mounted on the wall type, with a cord linking the handset to the dial assembly. He stared at it, wondering who should get the call. His mom lived in another state, and he still hadn't told her about his separation from Jenny. She was planning to visit next month, mostly to see Nate. I guess I better let her know she should reconsider her visit, he thought.

He had been driven for two hours in the back of a police car. A new experience for him—no sirens, no flashing lights. Just a quiet ride up the turnpike, with no conversation, as Sam's minimal criminal law training had him invoking his right to counsel before they had even placed him in the car. The officers were respectful, not saying a word to him during the ride, avoiding any mention of the murder charge.

The silence gave him time to reflect, but no clarity on why he was being accused of killing Gina's husband. He wanted to talk to her, to look her in the eye and explain that it was all a terrible misunderstanding, that he would never hurt her or her family. It sounded absurd, like something out of a soap opera, which he realized his life was turning into.

They'd taken his phone before putting him in the squad car. Not that they would've let him use it, but he'd wanted to check it, to see if anyone had tried to reach him. Now, all he could do was stare at the jail phone, his mind blank as he wondered who he could call. The choices were slim. The duty officer at the desk eyed him, as though her shift were more important than his moment of crisis.

He grabbed the handset and dialed the only number he could think of—Jenny. This should be so much fun, he thought bitterly. She's going to love hearing how I got arrested—if she picks up. Maybe she's out with Bill Harkins. Having a drink, maybe planning to get it on with him. He shoved the negative thoughts aside and dialed, his fingers moving slowly on the rotary. When was the last time I used a rotary phone? When's the next time I'll get to use my cell again?

"Hello?" Jenny's voice was hesitant.

"Jenny, it's me, Sam."

"Oh, Sam. Glad you called. I wanted to confirm you're picking up Nate tomorrow. Does five work for you?" In the background, the television blared. He figured she was grabbing a quick workout while Nate played in the next room.

"Jenny, I can't. I need to talk. . ."

She cut him off, her voice turning angry.

"Damn it, Sam. I can't rely on you for anything. I make plans, knowing I'll get some free time when you have him."

Guilt crept into Sam's gut. "I'm sorry. It's going to be difficult for me to get him."

"I know it's difficult. It's been difficult for me, too. But you can't just flake on me every time you're supposed to take Nate."

He wanted to argue that she was the one who flaked—who walked out on him—but this wasn't the time. "Jen, hold on. Listen for a minute. This isn't what you think."

She took a slow breath. The background noise died down, and Sam could hear her slowing her pace on the elliptical. At least, she wasn't ranting. "Go ahead," she said.

"I'm in trouble. Big trouble. I need your help." His voice trembled.

The noise on her end ceased. The television clicked off, and the sound of the exercise machine stopped. He imagined her standing still, sweat dripping, biting her lip to hold back her anger.

"What is it, Sam? Why do you suddenly need my help?" Her tone, though calmer, was still tinged with frustration.

He stumbled over his words before blurting, "I'm in jail. I'm in trouble."

"You're in jail? Why are you in jail? Were you drinking?" She sounded incredulous.

"No." He wanted to avoid sounding defensive. "I've been arrested for murder."

"Murder?!" Her voice rose with disbelief. "What the hell is going on?"

"I don't know." Sam wanted to cry, or at least complain, but he knew she wouldn't be in a sympathetic mood. "I can't explain it."

After a long pause, one that felt like an eternity, she asked, "What can I do to help?"

"That's the problem. I don't know. I couldn't think of anyone else to call."

"We'll figure this out. I'm sure you haven't done anything." Her tone had softened.

"Thanks. It's true. But I need a lawyer."

"Yes, you do."

"I need to talk to Gregg. Can you reach him for me?"

"Yes. Good idea. He'll know what to do."

"I hope." He gathered his thoughts. "Jen, I really appreciate you helping me. I don't know what this is about, but thank you for being there."

"Of course. We'll figure this out."

He glanced at the officer, who looked bored, but Sam knew his time was nearly up. "Jen, I have to go. Please let Gregg know what's happening. I need to talk to him as soon as possible."

As he hung up, a wave of panic engulfed him, like being sucked under the ocean by a massive swell. He froze, unable to move. After a moment, it passed, and he was left drained, sweat soaking his clothes. With so many questions unanswered, he had no idea what to do next.

Chapter 27

G REGG WORE HIS BEST suit to the penitentiary. Sam deserved that. Jenny had called him the night before, breathless, crying, and unable to explain much other than Sam had called from jail in another county and was being charged with murder.

With a little luck and a few calls to some police officers he knew, Gregg found Sam's arrest file online and gained some insight into what he was up against before arriving. Still, he had more questions than answers and needed to see what gaps Sam could fill in.

The facility was familiar to him, having visited many times for some of his more menacing clients. Being a criminal defense attorney meant representing some of the worst people society creates—murderers, rapists, and thieves. Most had no remorse for the bad acts they'd committed, nor any concern about committing more. It wasn't his job to judge them or to convince them of the wrongs of their ways, only to defend them and seek the most appropriate sentence under the circumstances.

He had little illusion that virtually every client he met with would end up in jail, either through a negotiated plea agreement or after a trial. Like every other criminal defense attorney, he'd scored few acquittals. They were guilty. He knew it. They knew it. His job was to fight against a system with little tolerance for the type of people he represented and to do his best to secure some portion of their lives outside of the penal system after they'd completed their debt to society.

He walked from his car carrying his briefcase, looking up at the towering walls topped with razor wire that glinted in the sunlight. A couple of guards walked along the tops of the walls, decked out in full riot gear and armed with high-powered rifles. The steel-and-concrete structure gave no illusions of comfort, impressing on anyone venturing inside that its primary purpose was to protect those outside from its residents. Every detail, from the smooth barricades to the security cameras mounted on every surface, suggested that its inhabitants would not infect those who had not chosen a violent, criminal path.

Each visit here reminded Gregg that this was not a place of rehabilitation but one of despair, where time moved slowly and painfully, and inmates had nothing to look forward to except a brief walk outside and occasional letters from home. Places like this, where the dregs of society congregated, were designed to crush souls, and only a few survived without deep, permanent emotional scars.

The amazing part to Gregg was that this wasn't even the worst of the prisons in the state system. Tucked away in more secluded areas were facilities housing even higher-level criminals, with more security, and even less hope for redemption.

It took him almost half an hour to get through security, resenting, though understanding, the need to remove everything from his pockets and take off his jacket, tie, belt, and shoes. Once he passed through the scanner, three guards escorted him through a series of dank, narrow hallways and locked doors until they arrived at the visitation room—a small, sterile space with bare, once-white walls, lit by harsh fluorescent fixtures.

Behind him, a heavy door closed with a thud, followed by the metallic ping of the lock engaging, signaling he would be trapped in the room until a guard let him out. The air was stale, tinged with the faint scent of disinfectant, which did little to mask the odor of sweat and despair that permeated the facility.

He had been in similar rooms hundreds of times before, consulting with clients, but this time, this meeting had no parallel for him. Behind the table sat Sam, shackled and unable to move, his head bowed, refusing to look up when Gregg took his seat.

In contrast to the stylish suits Sam liked to wear, today he wore a standard-issue orange jumpsuit that sagged at his shoulders and, true to its intent, made him appear formless. Before pulling out his yellow pad, Gregg reached forward and pressed his hand against the glass separating them. Sam made no movement in response.

"Hey, buddy. How's it going?" Gregg said through the microphone, flashing an ironic smile.

Sam kept his head lowered and said nothing.

"We have to talk, and I only have ten minutes before they kick me out. I know this is rough, but I'm not here as a friend. I'm here as an attorney, but only if you want me to represent you."

For the first time, Sam's eyes lifted from the table and locked on Gregg. His eyes were a moist pool of misery. He nodded. "I do," he said, his voice a raspy, almost inaudible whisper. "I need your help."

Gregg shifted forward, leaning into the conversation. "I'm not here to mince words or sugarcoat anything. You're in prison. You've been charged with murder. We've got a lot of work ahead of us."

Sam's eyes cleared, and his voice steadied. "I didn't do anything. This is crap. I don't know why they think I killed this guy."

"I get it, but now's not the time to dive into the details. I just want you to understand what's going to happen and what we need to do."

"Fine. Go ahead."

Gregg raised one finger. "First, there will be an arraignment. It's a formality, but you'll be taken to court for the judge to read the charges the State has filed against you. You can plead either 'guilty' or 'not guilty' to the charges. You'll plead 'not guilty.'"

"No shit. Keep going."

"There will also be a bail hearing. I'd like that to happen at the same time as the arraignment. In a case like this, I presume the court, if it even sets bail, will make it so high you'll have almost no chance of posting bond."

"You can't get me out of here?" Sam's voice strained as the reality of a lengthy incarceration hit home.

"Let's talk about that before the hearing. We'll have time to discuss it. There's nothing I can do about it now." Gregg rotated his neck to relieve some tension. "Not much happens quickly after that. We can engage in discovery. We'll get all the evidence the State has against you. They're required to give us everything they have, both good and bad. We'll have a clearer idea of what their case is about and how strong it is."

"What do we have to give them?"

"We don't have to give them anything. They won't talk to you. You won't say a word to them."

"I have no intention of talking to them."

"Smart. In fact, don't talk to anyone about your case. You never know who might be a snitch. You're not locked up with a bunch of boy scouts."

"Haven't met any yet."

"The court will set a trial date after the arraignment. Judges are under pressure to clear their dockets and schedule trials without delay, usually within a year of the charges. That sounds like a lot of time, but it's not."

"I want this over as soon as possible. I don't care if it's next week. I want to get this done."

"I understand, but there's a ton to do between now and trial. Remember, the State might offer us a plea deal."

"Not a chance," Sam said, slamming his hand onto the wooden ledge in front of him. "I didn't do anything. No deals."

Gregg held up a hand. "I get it. I'm not suggesting you should. I'm just laying out the path we're on and what might happen along the way."

"Sorry, go ahead."

"Don't apologize. Keep asking questions. You'll need to be involved in your defense." He paused to assess Sam. Once satisfied he was engaged, he continued, "I'll have a lot of motions to file. Motions to suppress evidence, motions to dismiss charges. There will also be a ton of investigation—talking to witnesses, getting experts. I have an investigator who will help me."

"That's a lot to do. I'm not sure how I'm going to pay you."

Gregg smiled. "You took care of me for my case. Never thought of charging me a dollar. Same deal here. You get my services, whatever they may be, for free."

"This is way more involved. You can't afford to do this for nothing."

"You can't afford not to let me. My practice is doing well. I can handle this. You have enough to worry about without thinking about finances. We're friends, and I want to make sure we handle this and get you out of here."

Sam's face flushed with color. He bit his lip. "I don't know what to say."

"Don't try. Like I said, you need to keep your head on a swivel in this place. Don't talk to too many people. Don't talk about your case. Keep yourself clean."

"Got it. Man, you have no idea how much I appreciate this."

Gregg nodded and then gathered his materials. As he stood to leave, he said, "I'll be in touch. A lot. It's my job to handle your worry."

He turned to walk toward the door and saw two guards lifting Sam to lead him away. Gregg never wanted to leave a room faster.

Chapter 28

FOR TWO DAYS FOLLOWING Gregg's visit, Sam spent most of his time in his cell, alone, with little to do but ponder his future. He had been placed in solitary confinement upon his arrival due to the nature of the charges against him. So far, the other inmates had paid him no attention, and without the opportunity to interact with many people, his focus remained fixed on his plight.

The previous day, the guard assigned to his wing—a hulking man with a square jaw who communicated more with grunts than words—had informed him that Jenny would be visiting the next day. The news forced him to contemplate every aspect of his life, preventing him from sleeping at all. Not that sleep had come easily recently; he was facing a murder charge and had to listen to the strange sounds echoing down his block at night once the lights were out.

At some point mid-morning—time was losing all meaning—the guard returned to his cell to escort him to meet Jenny. It took more than an hour to chain him, search him, and then lead him, with the assistance of two other immense guards, to the same room where he had met with Gregg.

She sat with her hands in her lap, in the same spot where Gregg had spoken to him the last time he had been brought here. Not giving much thought to what she should wear for a prison visit, she wore a dainty sundress with bare shoulders. The light streaming through the small, escape-proof window at the top of the room provided cinematic backlighting, giving her an angelic glow.

With three uniformed guards surrounding him, their obvious intent to harm him if he did anything unexpected, Sam avoided making eye contact with Jenny. She, however, wouldn't stop staring at him, concern, perhaps pity, etched on her face. She didn't try to make light of his situation, her nose scrunching up towards her eyes. "Are you okay?"

He had no reason to soften his response. He shook his head. "I'm so scared."

"What can I do?"

"I don't know. Thanks for getting ahold of Gregg. He was here. I guess you knew that."

She smiled. "He let me know you were doing okay. I want to help."

He leaned forward, causing his chains to clank against the floor. "I need your help. I'm not sure how or when, but I need it."

"I know we're in a weird situation," she said, her eyes welling. "You're still my husband. I will be there for you. Whatever you need. I will come to visit. I'll bring you anything you want." She looked at him, biting her lower lip. "Somehow, I feel like this is my fault. Like if I hadn't. . .," she trailed off, unable to find the words. "If I hadn't made you leave, this wouldn't have happened."

A mixture of conflicting emotions swirled inside him. In a moment's time, images of meeting Jenny, Nathan's birth, and her kicking him out flashed through his mind. He shook his head. "This has nothing to do with you. I don't know why I'm here, but you had nothing to do with whatever is happening." But as he said this, doubt crept into his consciousness. Had he been living at home, everything might have been different.

She stared at him with wide, unblinking eyes—a shade of blue deeper than he remembered. He recognized this look, the one she wore when she felt a deep connection with him and sought a stronger bond. Strange timing for this, but he didn't try to stop her.

He stared back at her. "I appreciate you being here, and whatever support you can offer will be a huge help. But I want you to understand, I don't know why I'm here. I didn't do anything. I don't know what you'll hear while I sort this out, but I can't have you thinking I did what they say I did."

Her eyebrows shifted only slightly, betraying some fleeting thought, but her gaze never wavered. "You don't have anything to worry about with me. There hasn't been a moment when I thought any of this is real. I can't imagine why they're saying you did this, but I don't think it's true. It's some kind of mistake, right?"

"Of course it is. They have nothing on me. Once I'm out of here, Gregg says we're going to sue them for unlawful prosecution. I can't wait."

She stood. "It's time. Whatever you need, I'm here for you. We'll fight this together."

Sam didn't know how to respond. He had already learned in prison that it's difficult to express emotion. He'd only been behind bars for a couple of days, yet he was beginning to understand the unspoken rules: don't say much, don't look at people, try not to be seen.

As Jenny walked toward the exit, once again, he watched his previous life fade away. His primary urge was to scream, but he sat there without moving a muscle.

Chapter 29

THE COURTROOM WAS FILLED with the families of the desperate. One by one, the accused were brought in, most shackled in some form, a parade of dirty orange jumpsuits. Jenny had planted herself in the back row two hours earlier. Sam's arraignment was scheduled for that time, but she hadn't realized the court would schedule twenty other arraignments for the same slot.

At least seven had already taken place. She was losing track, as each was a repeat of the last: the defendants dragged in by guards to confer with their attorneys. From her vantage, each defendant was a person of with little means—one woman so far—who met with a court-appointed lawyer for thirty seconds before standing before the judge to enter a plea. Each one entered a "not guilty" plea, and after a brief discussion, the judge would set bail. Jenny presumed none of them would be able to meet bail and would end up behind bars until trial.

Like a factory churning out widgets, the proceedings moved in preordained steps. Guards walked one defendant out while another set brought in the next. The bailiff announced the name of the defendant and the associated docket number. A group of three public defenders hovered at the side, one stepping forward to handle the next plea.

The entire process lacked humanity.

The charges the judge read ranged from petty theft to assault to the rape of a minor. To Jenny, however, what led to these charges didn't matter. Everyone was already guilty. The judge appeared so bored with the proceedings, as if he had seen the same thing day after day. She could see it in his eyes—they all had done it. They all deserved to go to jail.

As the parade continued, Gregg, sitting in the first row, turned and nodded to her. Sam's arraignment would be next.

Her pulse raced.

The bailiff yelled. *"Commonwealth v. Jordan.* Case number 4352." He handed a thin manila folder to the judge, who tossed it in front of him.

The side door opened again, and Sam was brought in by two guards, his hands cuffed at his waist. The jumpsuit he wore seemed to sag more than the last time she had seen him in prison, just ten days earlier. He looked toward the back of the courtroom and caught her eye. She managed a meager wave.

Gregg stood to greet Sam and guided him to the counsel table in front of the judge.

At the same time, the side door near them opened, and in walked a tall, striking woman dressed in a dark suit with a single-breasted jacket and a notched lapel. Underneath, she wore a crisp white blouse. Her low-heeled pumps clicked on the marble floor as she strode to the table next to Gregg. She faced forward without acknowledging his presence.

"Good morning, Your Honor. Marcia McBride, Elk County District Attorney."

The judge smiled for the first time. "It's always a pleasure to see you, Ms. McBride. We rarely get the county DA here."

The District Attorney's sudden appearance jolted Jenny. For the previous arraignments, a rookie assistant DA had handled the case. It didn't take much experience to ask the court to deny bail.

The judge nodded at Gregg, who stood. "Greggory Hubbard for the defendant." The judge waved his pen without looking up.

The judge picked up the folder, grabbed the indictment, and read it like he was ordering at a restaurant. "Mr. Jordan, you are charged with one count of first-degree murder, one count of second-degree murder, and one count of manslaughter. How do you plead?"

Sam stood with Gregg, who placed a hand on his back for support. "Not guilty, Your Honor." His voice sounded weak and unsure.

"Noted," Denby said after scribbling on the paper and handing it back to the bailiff. "What about the matter of bail?"

McBride stood. Her long waves of hair and small-hooped earrings framed her face. She stood a bit shy of six feet tall and looked at Gregg almost eye-to-eye. She directed her remarks to the judge. "This case involves a brutal, cold-blooded murder, the first here in six years. I am bound to protect the interests of the county's citizens. The evidence we will present will be overwhelming and will establish the defendant's guilt. Given the gravity of the crime, this court should not allow him on the streets. No bail should be set."

Gregg jumped to his feet. "That's ridiculous. The defendant has been improperly charged and poses no threat to anyone. He has no record—no jaywalking, no assaults, and certainly nothing similar to the crime he's accused of committing. He is a pillar of his community and gainfully employed. He needs to work to support his family. All he wants is to clear his good name."

"The defendant doesn't live with his family, and the wife is also employed, able to support their child." McBride smirked.

"He has never committed a crime. He is not a flight risk. Bail should be set so he doesn't rot in jail while waiting for trial."

"Tell that to his victim," McBride muttered, causing the judge to frown at her.

"Enough," the judge snapped. "I've heard enough. This is a first-degree murder case. I don't set bail in first-degree murder cases. The defendant has speedy trial rights. Bail denied. Next case."

The two guards approached Sam, who stood and walked behind them toward the door, disappearing like a plume of smoke on the other side. Gregg nodded at Jenny, directing her to meet him in the hallway.

Once there, he grabbed her arm, eyes wide. "The DA never tries cases. Something's going on here. I suspected an ADA would handle the arraignment. She wants to make a statement."

Jenny extricated herself from Gregg's grip and tugged at his suit jacket. "Is this a problem?"

"I don't know, but I don't like the message they're sending. This is a smaller county, and the politics are different. I'll figure this out. Don't worry."

She shook her head. "This all worries me."

Chapter 30

T HE PRACTICE OF LAW had never been about principles for Gregg. He was not one of those who, in law school, ran around spouting how much they loved the law. After graduation, he took a job with Pittsburgh's District Attorney's office. The goal was not to ensure wrongdoers paid their debts to society or that victims of crime received retribution.

Instead, he wanted to gain experience trying cases from the start, and the best way to get cases in front of juries immediately was to become a prosecutor. He assumed that with a wealth of trial experience, he would be able to write his own ticket after a couple of years and never have to worry about money again.

His intuition proved accurate.

He worked his way up from handling petty thefts to assaults and batteries, and eventually to the sex crimes unit. After his exposure to these types of cases, he had enough experience to become an attractive candidate for criminal defense firms in town.

He accepted a position at his current firm and realized that although he might have to offer lip service to principles, his primary focus would be on finding clients who were willing and able to pay his firm's hefty hourly rates. Now, he represented large corporate clients accused of white-collar crimes or other acts of corporate malfeasance.

He also handled cases for certain high-net-worth individuals who didn't flinch at his bills, often paying them with cash brought to the office in paper bags. He didn't ask questions about the source of the funds and had the office manager accept the payments to avoid touching the money.

Representing Sam was a new experience for him. It wasn't about the money because he wasn't taking any from him. It wasn't like he never did pro bono work. Often, he would take on indigent cases that the court sent over, but he did this to score points with the judges. Those were always lost causes, and despite his best efforts, those people, without fail, ended up back in jail.

He wouldn't let that happen to Sam.

The appearance of the District Attorney at Sam's arraignment had unsettled him. He had assumed they would have nothing compelling to link Sam to the murder. Still, he had yet to receive any of the evidence the State had gathered up to that point.

The day after the arraignment, he spent hours researching the murder. A few news articles popped up, but he didn't find much helpful information. The victim had been killed in his bed—two gunshots--one to the head and one to the chest. Some lurid crime scene photos had made it onto the internet, but he knew he would receive more gruesome photographs once the prosecution turned its evidence over to him. Police investigators always took numerous pictures of the deceased, documenting the wounds, the blood splatter, and he was sure would focus on the brain matter on the walls.

At this point, Gregg had no idea what connection, if any, Sam had to the victim, other than he was the husband of their old camp friend, Gina Szeka. He was scheduled to meet with Sam in a couple of days to discuss the charges and possible defenses. It would be the first of many meetings where they would go over the evidence, and, if necessary, prepare for trial.

It wasn't unusual for him to feel lost at the start of a case, knowing only the allegations against his client and not yet having access to the prosecution's evidence to prove guilt. That imbalance didn't last long, as prosecutors were required to turn over their evidence. Gregg was eager to get his hands on it so he could start testing it.

He called Marcia McBride with an invitation to discuss what she had. The District Attorney had been friendly, perhaps a bit condescending, but invited him to her office for an in-person meeting. He jumped at the opportunity, hoping to gain a better understanding of the case against Sam.

The two-hour drive allowed Gregg to reflect on the case. The main issue in his mind was how Sam could be connected to the victim. Sam had informed Gregg of his recent conversations with Gina, as well as their dinner together, but Gregg was still unaware of any connection Sam might have had with the deceased. Gregg contacted his investigator, a former Marine OPs guy who had worked with him for years, to determine if there was any connection between Sam and the victim, other than being Gina's husband. If it existed, his PI would find it.

By the time he pulled into the parking lot next to the courthouse, Gregg still had no clearer understanding of what connection Sam had to the murder than when he had started the drive. The two-dollar charge for all-day parking made him chuckle, especially in comparison to the twenty-five bucks it cost him back home. He grabbed his briefcase and headed inside, passing through the metal detector and down the main hallway until he reached the District Attorney's office.

He had been in numerous DA's offices across the state. Those in big cities bustled with assistants and investigators yelling to each other as attorneys scrambled to handle substantial caseloads ranging from petty crimes to rapes, murders, and child abuse. They were the same types of cases Gregg handled, just from the other side.

In smaller counties like this, the offices were quieter, staffed with only a few attorneys who dealt with DUIs and disorderly conduct cases, which made up the bulk of their caseload. Although these simple matters might make their way onto the back pages of the local newspaper, only in rare instances would a trial in this courthouse ever make the front page.

Back home, the DA would never meet with him on a case. His communications would go through the attorney handling the matter. The DA may have headed the office, but he was more of a politician than a trial attorney and relied on the experience of the office's other attorneys. DAs in smaller counties, though still politicians, often were more involved in handling specific cases.

Gregg pulled open the wooden door with a glass window etched with the District Attorney's name in bold, stenciled letters and entered the office. Within minutes, a petite, wholesome, young woman led him back to Marcia McBride's office. He appreciated her promptness.

McBride stood by her door with her hand extended as Gregg approached. After the perfunctory handshake, Gregg followed her inside while the receptionist closed the door behind them.

The office was immense, trimmed with wood on every wall, including well-maintained crown molding on the ceiling. An imposing picture window behind her desk offered a view of the town square and let in an abundance of natural light. Framed pictures of the DA glad-handing dignitaries and constituents lined the walls, drawing his eye to her diplomas grouped on a far wall. The furniture gleamed. He assumed she reveled in holding meetings here.

"Mr. Hubbard," she began. "Thanks so much for coming up here today. It looks like we will be spending a significant amount of time together."

He nodded. "I appreciate you inviting me here to discuss the matter. I hope we can jump right in."

"Of course. What would you like to discuss?"

Shifting in his chair, he said, "I want to talk about your prosecution of my client. What evidence do you have that links him to the murder?"

She turned in her seat, tilting her head and offering a smile. "I'm not prepared to discuss specifics at this point, but you're aware of the connection between Mr. Jordan and the victim's wife?"

"Connection? They were friends a long time ago and recently reconnected. That's not much of a connection."

"Perhaps, but I believe we can establish a much more meaningful connection. A more longstanding, intense one."

"If you have any evidence, then give it to me."

"Don't worry. I'll provide everything. Incriminating and exculpating. We do things by the book around here. We're sending it all out for investigation. Blood and ballistics. We'll send the reports once we have them."

"Only because you have to."

"Nah, I like you." She reached out and tapped his hand. "I'd give everything to you even if the rules didn't make me." She gave him a quick wink.

He didn't return the smile. Flirting with the person trying to put his friend in jail was near the bottom of his list of priorities.

The prosecutor, however, seemed to enjoy the game. She crossed her legs, exposing well-toned calves. She ran a finger up the front of her stockings. "Damn, got a run. These are brand new. Guess I'll have to buy some more before trial."

Gregg gave her a quizzical look. He couldn't figure out where she was coming from.

"Trial," she said. "You know, juries. Opening statements. Cross-examinations. Ends with a guilty verdict. Defendant goes to jail."

Gregg wanted to stop the theatrics. "Why did you invite me up here? We're not getting anywhere."

She gave him her best coy smile. "I just thought we should talk. We'll be spending lots of time together, and I want you to like me. I can be a pain in the ass in court. I wanted you to understand where I'm coming from before the festivities began."

"Festivities?"

"Yes. I'm looking forward to it." Then, without moving any other part of her body, her face lost all expression, and any pretense of rapport with Gregg evaporated. "You want the truth?" she continued. "The reason I wanted you to come here is to tell you I will not authorize any plea bargain in this case. None. We are going to trial. After you've had a chance to review the evidence we provide, I suggest you not waste our time attempting to get a deal for your client. It's not going to happen."

Gregg's head spun, like his first time in court. "Why? Every prosecutor wants to save time and money and get a plea. What's so different about this?"

The smile returned to her face, but there was no humor behind it—just a politician's skill at masking her true feelings. "Let me give you some of my backstory. Top of my class in law school. Worked at a big firm in New York for six years, but didn't like it. Came back home a couple of years ago and opened my own shop. Rubbed elbows with some of the bigwigs around here and they helped me get elected DA last year. I'm thirty-five, and it's time to move on to bigger things. It's nice here, but it's here, and I can only take so much farming country and lemonade."

She leaned forward toward Gregg. "So, one of our state's senators is retiring next year. I met him a while ago, and he suggested

I run for his seat. But he told me he'd only support me if I made a bigger name for myself. Well, I'm tired of prosecuting the two-bit crimes in this county. But then came our murder. Lots of blood, gore, and, as I think you're about to find out, the allure of sex. The national news is already sniffing around. Putting the murderer away for a long time will do wonders for my resume."

"You want to use this case to make a name for yourself?"

"Of course. Once your client is sentenced, everyone will be talking about the young, perky prosecutor who put him away. Once they know my name, that'll be my ticket to getting the senator's support."

"What if you lose?"

She laughed. "An experienced prosecutor knows her case and won't try one she thinks she might lose. That's me." She winked again, which Gregg took as his cue that the meeting was over.

He stood. "Well, I guess we're in for a fight. When your political career goes up in smoke, let's have dinner and discuss how you overplayed your hand."

He turned without saying goodbye and stormed out of the office. Once outside, he bent over and put his hands on his knees to stop his body from shaking.

Chapter 31

THE PRISON WHERE SAM now spent his days was a twenty-minute drive from the Elk County courthouse. If his case were to go to trial, he would be moved to the county facility next to the courthouse, where he would spend his days in trial and his nights in confinement.

So far, Gregg had not had the heart to tell Sam that if he were convicted, he would be transferred to a more secure facility in the middle of the state. No matter how bad Sam viewed his current situation, the other place would be so much worse.

After meeting with the District Attorney, Gregg made a beeline for the prison. Without an appointment, the guards gave him a hard time when he announced his intention to visit his client. Despite their pushback, Gregg knew they would relent and fetch Sam.

It took an hour, giving Gregg space to sort through his thoughts on why his meeting with the DA had been so disconcerting. It wasn't just her attitude but also her unwavering confidence in her ability to prove Sam's guilt. Her flirtatious conduct, though mildly amusing, was still unsettling, as no self-respecting DA would act that way unless she had solid evidence pointing to Sam's involvement in the murder.

Gregg still hadn't seen the evidence that made her so giddy but needed to have a more in-depth conversation with Sam now, even though he knew the DA would send over everything soon enough.

After the pat-down and walk through the labyrinthine hallways, he was placed once again in the same meeting room as before, facing Sam, who scowled and displayed no sign that his lawyer's presence provided him any relief.

Gregg avoided pleasantries. "I just met with the DA. She's not messing around. She's coming straight for you and seems to relish the chance to put you away for a long time."

Gregg's quick summary wiped the smugness from Sam's face, leaving him with Gregg's full attention. "What are you talking about?" Sam asked.

"The DA wants your scalp. She thinks it'll boost her political career. Seems like she believes she's got you by the balls."

Sam's face lost all color. He spit out, "How? What?"

"I'm not sure what she has yet, but she's acting like she has it all." His voice lost its usual confidence. "What could she have?"

"I have no idea." Sam slumped. "I've told you before, Gina and I made contact. We flirted a little, but it was just going to be a fling. Nothing permanent. I went to have a second dinner with her, but she never showed. I went home and then found out her husband had been killed. I had nothing to do with it. I don't even know where she lives. Somebody's made a big mistake."

"Well, none of this looks good. You just reconnected with her. You planned to meet with her. You wanted to spend the evening with her, and then her husband ends up dead. That gives them motive, at the very least. If they have anything else connecting you to what happened, we need to have a much more serious conversation. Are they going to have anything?" His voice rose. "Tell me."

Sam shook his head, but he couldn't meet Gregg's gaze. He slammed his hand on the table, causing the shackles to clank. "No, there can't be anything else. I didn't do anything. I don't know her husband. I never met him." He raised his eyes and stared at Gregg but couldn't hide his fear.

"Are you sure?" Gregg raised his voice just loud enough to draw a glance from a guard. He paused, took a breath, and then whispered through clenched teeth, "What aren't you telling me?"

"Nothing. Absolutely nothing. You can prove I didn't do anything, can't you?"

Gregg looked up at the ceiling. "We don't have to prove anything. We just have to make sure they can't prove anything against you."

"How can they prove something if I didn't do anything?"

"You understand how it works. Truth at trial is all relative. It doesn't matter what's true; it's what you can prove and whether the jury believes it. Reality doesn't matter. If you can make a jury believe it, you can say anything."

Sam looked more desperate. He leaned forward. "Truth has to matter."

Gregg shook his head. "You're not that naïve, are you?"

"I believe the truth wins out in the end. I have to." Sam's eyes widened.

"You've tried a lot of cases. One side says one thing happened, the other side says the opposite, and the truth is somewhere in the middle. That's what you've told me." He paused, ensuring Sam was listening. "Let me tell you something about the sexual harassment case you handled for me. You remember it? It wasn't too long ago."

Sam nodded.

"Well, everything Amy Chokra said was true."

Sam raised his eyebrows. "What are you talking about?"

"She was telling the truth. Pretty much every word. I just got on the stand and bluffed. She couldn't prove what she was saying, and I made the arbitrators doubt her by speaking with confidence and never wavering during my testimony."

"You had me represent you and tell a complete fabrication?"

"You didn't do anything wrong. That was on me. I'm only telling you now because the truth didn't matter in that case. She needed proof, but she couldn't prove anything. I'm only thinking about your well-being, not the truth. I want you to understand that the truth may be with you, but if you can't prove it, it doesn't do you any good. I'm worried the DA must think she has proof of something, because she was so eager to meet with me."

"I've told you, they can't have anything on me because I didn't do anything."

"And I'm telling you, I'm concerned about what they might have."

"What about reasonable doubt?"

"What about it? Yes, they must prove their case beyond a reasonable doubt. But lots of innocent people are rotting away in jail after being convicted based on proof that may not have been beyond a reasonable doubt."

"Just tell me what I need to do."

"Don't worry. I will. For now, keep thinking about everything that happened the night you went to meet her for dinner. Something in those details is going to help." Gregg reached out toward Sam. "I've got to go. We'll talk after I get their evidence. Stay safe."

A weak smile crossed Sam's face as his friend walked out of the room.

Chapter 32

G REGG'S OFFICE, PALATIAL COMPARED to the digs he occupied during his years as an assistant DA, was on the thirty-fifth floor of a high-rise planted right in the middle of downtown, across from the courthouse. From his desk, he had a perfect view of the square in front of the court complex. He often watched people scurry up the steps or observed energized groups demonstrating with picket signs in the plaza.

So much different from the sleepy town where Sam's trial would take place, but the venue didn't matter. Whether the courthouse was pristine or showed cracks from years of dilatory maintenance, all that mattered were the twelve people sitting in the jury box and the decision they rendered.

Gregg spent most of his time across the street handling pleas, arguing pre-trial motions, and representing clients at their trials. During his years representing the government, he, like many of his colleagues, justified the pitiful pay to friends by reminding them how he was putting scum in jail, and making sure they didn't harm people who would never consider committing a crime. The reality, however, was that he was biding his time until a swanky defense firm swooped in, hired him, and started paying him like a real attorney.

Like many of his buddies from the DA's office, he could rationalize his limited ability to spend money for only so long. When he went to happy hour with his law school pals who worked at big corporate firms, he was the only one who worried about paying fifteen bucks for a drink because he was the only one whose salary wasn't in six figures—nowhere close.

He often started a joke by saying that leaving the DA's office to represent the other side offended his sense of justice and morality. The punchline? "That lasted until I received my first paycheck from my new firm." It was almost three times what he had made representing "the people," which made the switch much easier to stomach.

In an instant, even those he had once referred to as "scum" while on the prosecution's side were now entitled to fundamental Constitutional rights and deserved quality representation. In the blink of an eye, he justified doing everything in his power to get his clients off, railing against the dirty tricks prosecutors played.

And he slept like a baby in his new condo, bought soon after entering private practice. Perhaps he compromised some of his long-held values, but he stopped worrying about making his next car payment.

The firm he worked for was small, with just five lawyers, but they had plenty of clients, most of whom had little difficulty paying three hundred bucks, or more, an hour for their legal services. He always got paid upfront because people who ended up in jail didn't care about settling up with their attorneys. And despite their best efforts, most of their clients ended up serving time.

Gregg sat by his computer, waiting for an email from Marcia McBride, who had called earlier that morning to tell him to expect the State's *Brady* material. Of course, that was after five minutes of understated flirting, where she talked about how attractive he was and wondered how form-fitting his suit would be at trial.

Elizabeth Liriano, the newest associate in his office, perched in front of his desk with a pen and yellow pad at the ready, staring at the computer screen.

"She said we would receive the materials by noon. It's five to," Gregg said, staring at his laptop. "We'll find out if her word's any good."

He waited a minute, but nothing came.

"What can we expect from her?" Liriano asked, breaking the silence.

Gregg forced his eyes away from his screen. "It should be everything they have to send us under the law. You just graduated from law school. I'm sure you studied *Brady*. What do they have to give us?"

She twirled her pen while looking up. "Under *Brady*, the government basically has the obligation to provide the accused with all its evidence, whether good or bad, prior to trial so the defendant can prepare an adequate defense to the charges brought against him."

"Correct. Don't use the word 'basically,' but that's right." He mumbled, "And don't say 'totally.' It's meaningless. What do they have to give us?"

"Pretty much everything they have. Like any witness statements, physical evidence, and expert reports. And, as I said, any exculpatory evidence—evidence that might help our side."

"Again, good answer. Stop saying 'like.'" He smiled.

She returned the smile. "She has one more minute." And as the words left her mouth, Gregg's computer dinged, signaling the receipt of an email. He gestured at it like he had just received the holy grail.

"Let's take a gander at what she's sent us."

He tapped on his keyboard, causing a zip file to appear on his screen. "Damn. There's like thirty different folders in here."

"You shouldn't say 'like,'" she mumbled.

Gregg didn't respond, staring straight ahead while opening the files, making document after document appear. A look of horror crossed his face.

"Shit, this is bad."

She moved around the desk and stared over his shoulder. "What is all that?"

"It might be the death knell of a friend of mine."

"There's so much."

"I know. They've identified witnesses we haven't heard of before. Tons of photographs. Expert reports. Here's one from Dr. Alan Whitmore, a renowned DNA expert with an international reputation. I don't like this."

Elizabeth moved away from the computer. "I can print all these off and we can go through everything. I'm ready to do whatever you want."

"This is bad," Gregg mumbled, leaning forward with both hands on his desk and shaking his head. He slapped his desk and muttered, "Shit, Sam, what the hell were you doing?"

Chapter 33

ELIZABETH LIRIANO HAD WORKED at Gregg's firm for three months since passing the bar. Her hire had raised eyebrows—not only because she had no experience as a criminal attorney, but because she had no prior legal practice of any kind. However, her exceptional résumé, boasting accolades like Law Review Editor and *Magna Cum Laude*, had opened doors typically closed to most graduates from her law school. During interviews, her near-photographic memory and ability to recite case law verbatim had left indelible impressions.

Despite offers from three of the city's most prestigious firms, Elizabeth approached Gregg's boutique criminal defense practice, captivating the three partners during her interview. Lawyers of her caliber usually gravitated toward the corporate giants or pursued clerkships with federal judges. But Elizabeth had a different vision for her career. She craved trial experience—specifically in criminal law. While she could have secured a position as an Assistant District Attorney, her salary expectations far exceeded what public service could offer.

Elizabeth successfully persuaded Gregg's firm to take a chance on her, making history as their first hire without prosecutorial experience and the first fresh law graduate to join their ranks. Within weeks, her meticulous research skills and impressive billing capacity had endeared her to the senior attorneys, who often vied for her input on creative strategies for court arguments. Her career trajectory seemed destined for success.

Now, with the trial for Sam Jordan looming, Elizabeth had meticulously organized every piece of evidence. Documents were digitized and printed, neatly stacked in the second-floor conference room. Unlike many of her peers, Elizabeth preferred reviewing hard copies, annotating them with highlighters. Gregg, recognizing her methods' effectiveness, had embraced this approach. Together, they had spent weeks poring over every document from the prosecution, repeatedly analyzing them and consulting experts nationwide.

However, the expert opinions they received were troubling. While some experts identified minor inconsistencies in the prosecution's evidence, they generally agreed with its conclusions, which painted a damning picture for their client. The experts if they were to testify would offer little to counter their core findings.

Gregg ran a hand through his hair as he combed through the files again, his frustration mounting. Elizabeth stood nearby, visibly disheartened, unable to uncover a critical flaw in the prosecution's case.

"I'm not seeing anything different," Gregg admitted, his voice strained. "I can't find any holes in their conclusions."

Elizabeth frowned, her frustration evident. "I've reviewed the prosecution's reports over and over. Their analysis feels wrong, but I can't pinpoint how. Based on your conversations with Mr. Jordan, their conclusions seem impossible."

Gregg exhaled sharply. "Exactly. I keep rereading them, and they're haunting my dreams. Even the simplicity of the ballistics report: 'Beyond a reasonable degree of certainty, I can opine that the defendant fired the weapon that killed Pablo Marcon.' Sam was nowhere near the scene, so how can their expert be so certain he pulled the trigger?"

Silence filled the room before Elizabeth grabbed another stack of papers, waving them as though they might hold the answer. "And the blood analysis report! It doesn't add up. These conclusions don't align with what we understand about the evidence." Her voice faltered.

"Or," Gregg said grimly, "maybe we don't actually understand the evidence. What if their experts have access to something we don't? It's like they're working off a completely different case."

Elizabeth stood straighter, determination flashing in her eyes. "So, what do we do?"

Gregg pushed his chair back and wandered to the window. He shoved his hands into his pockets, gazing out at the river below. A small motorboat buzzed along, its occupants laughing and holding beer bottles aloft. Gregg imagined them beckoning him to abandon the case and join their carefree revelry. He blinked the thought away.

"I don't know," he murmured, his voice barely audible. "Maybe we need to treat this as a hung jury case, not one for acquittal."

"You mean like focusing on reasonable doubt instead of telling our own story?" Elizabeth asked, raising an eyebrow.

"Exactly. But don't say 'like.' At this point, we don't even have a story. Sam's version doesn't align with the evidence. If we can't make sense of it, our best option may be to dismantle the prosecution's witnesses during cross-examination and hope the jury finds reasonable doubt. But let's not jump to conclusions yet. We need to keep working the evidence."

Elizabeth gave a small, encouraging smile. "I've already started drafting cross-examination outlines. There are a few promising angles we can exploit."

Gregg returned to his seat with a weary nod. "Let's hope they're enough. For Sam's sake, I really hope they're enough."

Chapter 34

GREGG WAITED IN HIS car for fifteen minutes before trudging up the sidewalk to ring the doorbell. Over the years, he'd had countless difficult conversations—poring over evidence, discussing plea deals with clients' families, and making life-altering recommendations. In most cases, he had no trouble being direct: outlining options, offering opinions, and preparing his clients for the difficult road ahead.

But this was different.

The previous night, Gregg had called Jenny, demanding a meeting to discuss Sam's upcoming trial. Separations, like as in Sam and Jenny's case, were not unusual for his clients, and it didn't lessen the importance of the discussion. Jenny needed to be ready for anything that might unfold in court—and, most importantly, she needed to know how to react. He also had to prepare her for the possibility of testifying, even if it was unlikely.

Jenny answered almost immediately after Gregg knocked, weariness etched on her face. She hugged him, strong and firm, and invited him inside.

Gregg wanted to dive straight into trial preparation mode, but sensed Jenny wasn't ready. "How are you holding up?" he asked.

She offered a forced smile that didn't mask her inner conflict. "I'm managing. How about you? Do you want some coffee?"

"I'm fine. Coffee would be great."

Jenny led him to the kitchen. He had been to the house many times, but today, it felt unfamiliar. Though little had changed, everything felt different. Jenny didn't glance back at him until they reached the coffee maker. She grabbed a mug. "Cream?"

"Just black," Gregg replied.

She shook her head. "Of course. I should've remembered."

They sat at the kitchen table, which overlooked the backyard. Nate was outside, swinging on a swing set. Gregg gestured toward the window. "How's he doing?"

Jenny bit her lower lip. "He's okay. He misses his dad."

Gregg nodded, pulling a stack of papers from his briefcase.

"You know," Jenny said, breaking the silence, "this is all my fault."

Gregg looked up, his brows furrowed. "Stop. This isn't your fault. I don't know who's to blame for this, but it's not you."

Jenny stood and began to pace around the room. "If I hadn't kicked him out, this never would've happened. If I'd been a better wife, he'd be here. Nate would be playing with him in the backyard." Her voice wavered as she glanced at her son, who was now spinning in circles and tumbling to the ground.

"Jenny, don't do this to yourself. No one can say what would've happened if Sam had stayed. We might still be in the same place."

She turned to him, a tear dancing down her cheek. "I got bored, and now he's paying the price."

Gregg stood and hugged her. He brushed a strand of hair from her face. "Whatever happened, you're not responsible. This is the last time you think or talk like that. Understand?"

She nodded, wiping her nose. "I get it. I know."

They retook their seats. Gregg set a yellow pad on the table and exhaled. "The trial's in three weeks. First, I need to know if you'll be there."

Jenny shot him a look. "If you tell me it's best for him, I'll be there."

"It is. Family presence sends a powerful message to the jury. Your support is crucial. I've spoken to his mom—she's coming. It'll be hard for her, but she's determined to be there as much as she can. His brothers, though, won't be attending."

"She's a strong woman," Jenny murmured. "I'll make sure she's okay. What should I do during the trial?"

"Hey, you're a lawyer. You know what's going to happen, but for now, I'm going to pretend like you have no idea what to expect." He took a sip of coffee. "With luck, you won't need to testify. You're not a witness to anything relevant, and I don't want to subject you to cross-examination. But if we decide otherwise, you'll have ample preparation."

Jenny nodded. "Of course."

"Your main role," Gregg continued, "is to present yourself as the devoted, supportive wife. Dress conservatively—like you're going to church. Nothing revealing and nothing too somber, though. We don't want to look defeated."

"I can handle the un-sexy, loving wife vibe."

Gregg smiled faintly. "I'm sure you can." His tone grew serious. "Jenny, I need you to understand how difficult this is going to be for you. The stress of sitting through a criminal trial can be overwhelming. It'll wear you down and wear you out. But no matter what happens, the jury can't see that anything might be affecting you. Every day, every minute, you'll need to maintain a stoic, supportive demeanor. No reactions, no matter what you hear."

Jenny frowned. "What do you mean? What might I hear?"

Gregg hesitated. "I don't want to go into specifics now, but the defense might reveal things about Sam's life after he moved out. Things you might not like or understand and find upsetting."

Jenny's face reddened. "Like what?"

"It's hard to say. We're reviewing his correspondence and texts. There may be... revelations about his state of mind or things he considered doing. The important thing is, if anything surprises you, don't react. Act like you expected it and it doesn't bother you. Make sense?"

Jenny nodded and took a deep breath. "The jury will see a devoted wife. I can handle it. I still care about Sam, and I'll do what's best for him. Not a problem."

Gregg gathered his papers and stood. "Thanks for the coffee." He placed his mug in the sink and turned to Jenny. "You understand how critical this is? Your presence and composure will make a difference for Sam." He gave Jenny a kiss on the cheek. "He'll need all the help you can give."

Jenny offered a faint smile. "Anything he needs. Just ask." She placed their mugs in the dishwasher, then leaned against the sink. She gazed out the window, watching Nate roll on the grass, laughing. Despite everything, she smiled.

Chapter 35

"**Y**OU'RE LOOKING RATHER HOT today, aren't you, sweet-ie?"

Marcia McBride's simple question, as deliberately inappropriate as it was, threw Gregg's equilibrium out of whack. She was the County's District Attorney, yet her incessant flirtation and innuendo left him as dizzy and disoriented as a first-time speeder caught red-handed.

Gregg had once again traveled two hours to discuss a serious case, not fend off suggestive comments. He tried to redirect the conversation. "I drove up here to talk about our case. The trial is coming up."

McBride feigned surprise. "What trial? Oh, I must have forgotten to put it on my calendar. What are we going to do with such an important trial?" She turned to her computer and typed with theatrical indifference. "Oh wait, I found it. I have it marked right here. It says, 'Trial with hot lawyer.' That's you, isn't it?"

Her words seemed to suck the air out of the room. Gregg struggled to respond. Witty retorts sprang to mind—'This attorney is too hot for you,' or 'Should we test how hot we both are?'—but this wasn't a bar. It was a meeting about a murder trial where she was seeking to imprison his friend for decades. The glib comebacks evaporated, and he forced himself to focus on discussing the trial.

"Ms. McBride, I'm here to go over pretrial motions and explore common ground for a potential plea agreement," Gregg said, handing her a folder. "I've spoken with Mr. Jordan, and he's willing to hear the government's position."

McBride opened the folder and skimmed its contents with the nonchalance of someone selecting salad dressings at the grocery store. Then, flashing her most radiant, "Vote for me" smile, she tossed the folder to the far edge of her desk.

"First, please call me Marcia. All my friends do," she said, pausing for a response that didn't come. "As for a plea deal, I believe I was clear in our previous meeting: my office won't be offering one. This case is going to trial. And between you and me, I expect the jury's verdict to give my political career quite the boost."

Gregg shook his head. "I've never handled a case where no plea was offered. You can't place Sam at the scene of the crime. He has no reason to commit the crime and, c'mon, you're an experienced attorney, juries are unpredictable. You know that. This case is riddled with reasonable doubt."

"I disagree. Once the jury hears from our experts, they'll have no doubt who committed the crime." She tilted her head. "So far, I haven't seen anything in your experts' reports that refutes our conclusions. No deal."

Gregg stood. "Then I guess I'll see you at the pretrial conference." He gestured toward the folder on her desk. "Once the judge reviews our motions and starts kicking out your evidence, you may want to revisit this discussion."

"Like I said, we're going to trial. Thanks so much for coming by to chat. Of course," she added with a smirk, "you could've just emailed me your motions—it would have been so much easier for you." Rising from her chair, she extended her hand. "I'm hopeful you and I are able to have a good time trying this case. I think you're going to find out that I'm rather fun and can be quite humorous. People say I have a dry sense of humor. Like a martini. Maybe after the trial we can grab one and see what else we have in common."

Gregg turned on his heel, once again at a loss for words. Outside, he slammed his briefcase into the backseat of his car, overwhelmed by the same convoluted frustration he'd felt the first time he met McBride. He suspected it wouldn't be the last.

Chapter 36

TWO FLAGS WAVED IN unison on the grounds of the Elk County courthouse. One, representing the United States of America whipped in the wind on one side of the cement walkway leading to the entrance, while the Commonwealth's flag mirrored its movements on the opposite side.

Gregg and Elizabeth Liriano, both dressed impeccably for court, walked past the flags without so much as a glance. His charcoal-gray suit radiated professionalism, while her bright blue attire nearly matched the hue of the cloudless sky.

Inside the courthouse, the morning sun filtered through large arched windows, casting intricate patterns of light and shadow to dance across the polished marble floors. The pair navigated their way to Judge Denby's courtroom and settled in the back row, arriving more than half an hour early for the pretrial conference.

Fifteen minutes later, the stillness of the nearly empty courtroom was interrupted by the arrival of Marcia McBride and her entourage. The District Attorney swept into the room, trailed by two young assistants burdened with bulging bags of legal documents. They made a beeline for their counsel table, meticulously arranging papers and writing tools.

McBride's spotted Gregg and Elizabeth at the back of the room. She strode toward them, her tailored navy-blue suit emphasizing her athletic build.

Gregg rose to greet her, reminding himself to maintain eye contact. Before he said a word, McBride said, "Damn, Gregg, you fill out a suit like you're posing for a magazine cover. I'm not sure I'll be able to focus with you flashing those threads."

He gestured toward Liz. "I'd like you to meet my associate, Elizabeth Liriano. She'll be assisting me during the trial."

McBride's smile widened as she shook Liz's hand. "Aren't you the lucky one? Working closely with my good friend Gregg. I bet you two are burning the midnight oil together. There's only one way I know to relieve that kind of stress."

Liz blinked, momentarily stunned by McBride's bluntness, before managing a polite nod.

Meanwhile, McBride's assistants, eager for approval, finished organizing the documents. McBride turned toward them briefly. "These are Sarah Nguyen and Jack Thompson," she said, nodding in their direction. "Two newly minted lawyers in my office."

The young lawyers shook hands with Gregg and Liz, murmuring in unison, "Pleasure to meet you."

"That's about all you'll hear from them," McBride quipped with a smirk. "This is my case. I'll handle all the witnesses and arguments. Their job is to make me look organized." She glanced at them again. "Did you write good briefs in response to the motions defense counsel has submitted?" They nodded without speaking. Gregg half-expected her to pat them on the head like obedient puppies.

Before the interaction could grow more awkward, the judge's clerk appeared at the door near the bench. "Please take your seats. Judge Denby will take the bench shortly."

The attorneys moved to their respective tables with the prosecution settling near the empty jury box, while Gregg and Liz sat at thet table further away. Moments later, Judge Denby entered through a side door, his black robe flowing near to the floor. Everyone in the room stood briefly before he waved them to sit.

"This is the pretrial conference for *Commonwealth v. Jordan*. Counsel, please enter your appearances for the record."

McBride stood first, confidently introducing herself and her team. Gregg followed, identifying himself and Elizabeth.

Judge Denby opened a folder. "Let's begin with the defense's motion to suppress evidence taken from the defendant's home. Mr. Hubbard, proceed."

Gregg stood, his voice steady. "Your Honor, items were seized from the defendant's former residence under a search warrant issued the previous evening. We had no opportunity to contest the warrant before the search. The property was no longer the defendant's primary residence, making the search improper based on the information provided."

Denby finished taking notes and turned to the prosecution. "Ms. McBride, your response?"

McBride stood, smoothing her blouse. "Your Honor, the defendant listed the searched address as his residence at the time of his arrest and had not updated his address elsewhere. The search was lawful and routine. Both my office and the officers acted within the bounds of the law."

The judge raised a hand to forestall further argument. "I've reviewed the briefs and find the search was valid. Evidence obtained will be admissible at trial."

He shuffled through the folder, producing another document. "Next, the defense's motion to dismiss the indictment on grounds of prosecutorial misconduct. Mr. Hubbard, please proceed."

Gregg grimaced before addressing the court. "Your Honor, the district attorney's office has repeatedly leaked information about this case to the press. The Elk Gazette has published articles every day for the past week with information it could only have received from the DA's office. In fact, just yesterday Ms. McBride had a thirty-minute press conference where she spoke at length about this case which, in all likelihood, our potential jurors would have heard, and which, if they did, would prejudice them against my client."

McBride shot to her feet. "Nothing published in the press deals with any of the facts of this matter. I simply stated that our office prosecutes cases based upon reasonable evidence and that no case will be brought unless a grand jury first issues an indictment. The public has a significant interest in this case and my office will always respect the integrity of the legal system."

Gregg muttered under his breath, "I'll bet you do."

The judge nodded, his lips pressing together. "I have reviewed each of the newspaper articles the defense has attached to its motion and have rewatched the prosecution's news conference. Although I believe it's better practice not to engage with the media at all, it does not appear the prosecution has stepped over any lines. As you can see from the reporters who are here today," he swept his hand across the courtroom at the four reporters in the back, "this case is generating significant interest. I will not deny the media's access to my courtroom but would instruct all parties not to try their cases in the press. With that said, the defense's motion is denied."

Turning to the attorneys, he asked, "Any further motions?" Both parties shook their heads.

"Very well," he concluded. "Jury selection begins Monday. This court stands in recess until then."

As Gregg and Liz exited the courtroom, McBride caught up. "Denby's tough, but fair," she said. "Let's hope he doesn't take out any of his frustrations on your pretty face." She reached to touch Gregg's face, who sidestepped her hand.

"Don't be like that," she laughed, striding away. "This trial's going to be fun. We all are going to have such a good time."

Gregg sighed. "Trying a case with that woman is going to be my downfall."

Liz nodded, releasing a long, weary breath.

Chapter 37

T HE DESIGN OF THE conference room in Gregg's office was meant to impress both current and prospective clients. A custom-made mahogany table, large enough to seat twelve, stretched down the center of the room. Its polished surface gleamed under the soft glow of ambient lighting. Surrounding the table were matching dark leather chairs, exuding elegance and professionalism. Expensive wall sconces adorned the walls, completing the refined atmosphere.

Amenities were thoughtfully scattered throughout the room: charging ports, a coffee station, and cabinets stocked with snacks and supplies. Every detail ensured that meetings could stretch on for hours without the need for external interruptions, whether for sustenance or technical assistance.

Yet, despite the comfort the room provided, Gregg and Liz grumbled as they finalized their trial preparations. For the past week, they had occupied this space almost continuously, leaving only for quick bathroom breaks or a few hours of restless sleep at home late at night.

Their files were meticulously organized. Every piece of evidence had been collated in triplicate—copies prepared for the court, the witnesses, and the court reporter. The documents were stored in neatly indexed boxes, ensuring instant retrieval and eliminating the risk of fumbling for a crucial page during trial. Even so, Gregg and Liz found themselves staring wearily at the rows of boxes.

Criminal defense lawyers were a breed apart. No matter how diligent the preparation, cases most often ended with defendants serving jail time. Success wasn't measured by wins or losses, but by unyielding preparation and the determination to leave no stone unturned—all while staying well within the bounds of ethics and the law.

For Gregg, the harsh reality of this work demanded emotional control, especially during trials where the odds overwhelmingly favored the prosecution. But this time, the stakes felt different. Sam was the accused, and Gregg couldn't suppress his raw emotions. Deep in the recesses of his mind, he couldn't shake the haunting image of Sam being led away in handcuffs.

Gregg had stood beside countless defendants as they faced the grim finality of a jury's decision. He had witnessed their shock, their disbelief, as the realization set in that they had failed to sway the jurors away from the prosecution's arguments. Now, a gnawing doubt crept into his thoughts—an insidious fear that he wouldn't be able to dismantle the prosecution's case. With immense effort, he forced those thoughts aside, refusing to picture Sam languishing behind bars.

Chapter 38

EVERY EVENING AT NINE, the cellblock lights dimmed, leaving only the faint glow of emergency canisters casting a shadowy hue into Sam's cell. Lying on his cot, he was alone with his thoughts. Since his incarceration, he hadn't feared for his physical safety. Strangely, no one had threatened him. In fact, he had barely spoken to any other inmates, leaving him without allies or enemies. He didn't worry about a jailhouse informant claiming he confessed to the murder—he hadn't had a conversation long enough for anyone to gain such leverage.

His emotional well-being was another matter. Time had become an unrelenting blur. Sam no longer knew what day it was or how long he had been in jail. His trial began the next day, and he stared at the ceiling, trying to steel himself for whatever the prosecution might present. The events of his dinner with Gina replayed in his head, as they had every night since. Yet, what once seemed vivid and enticing, memorable and distinctive, had become elusive. Had she said she wanted to leave her husband? Did they plan a second meeting? Was anything about her real?

Gregg had visited the prison several times to review the evidence and prepare Sam for trial. Together, they practiced potential direct examination questions and rehearsed mock cross-examinations. Sam knew his chances of testifying were slim. "Only as a last resort," Gregg had emphasized. "My job is to create enough doubt for the jury so you won't need to take the stand."

Yet doubt had already taken root in Sam's own mind, burrowing in deeper with each passing day since the cops dragged him from his office. Over time, the weight of others' suspicion had him questioning his own recollection of the events on the night of the murder.

Jenny visited regularly, never complaining about the drive or the fact that Sam was in prison. She followed Gregg's advice, doing whatever she could to make prison life more tolerable for Sam. Whether it was bringing food or sharing stories about Nate, her efforts brought brief moments of relief. Any smile she pried out of him affirmed her belief that she was helping.

Sam clung to every scrap of information about Nate, bombarding her with questions about his life. Any tidbit, any morsel, lifted his spirits. "He's kicking a soccer ball around the backyard," or "His teachers say he's so bright," would spark a cascade of follow-ups. Despite his longing to see his son, Jenny never brought Nate to visit. "I can't do that to him," she would say. Sam understood. If the trial didn't go his way, he might never see his boy again.

The thought of a guilty verdict haunted Sam more often now. Tonight, the image of a smug jury declaring him guilty filled his mind. He imagined their self-satisfied faces as they delivered the devastating verdict. He forced himself to focus instead on the closure the trial might bring. Nothing could be worse than the purgatory of waiting, except perhaps spending decades in a prison more dangerous and disgusting than the one he currently endured.

Sam picked up the dog-eared paperback on the tiny shelf next to his bed. The dim light allowed him to read, but his thoughts kept wandering. Shadows danced on the cell walls, long and sinister like arms reaching for him. Sleep remained elusive as ever, but he hoped tonight it would come at some point to provide an escape from his thoughts. Pulling the coarse, flimsy blanket over his head, he closed his eyes and willed rest to come.

Sleep came no easier for Jenny. At three in the morning, she crept downstairs, hoping that tidying the kitchen might quiet her restless mind. After placing the lone stray glass into the dishwasher, she realized there wasn't much more to straighten. She gave herself a small mental pat on the back for managing the house, raising her kid, and not losing her sanity at the same time her husband awaited trial for murder.

Her faith in Sam hadn't faltered. She believed him when he said the charges were baseless. Still, their future had been murky even before this. Time had been her ally, providing her with the space to decide whether to let Sam back into her life. Now, everything was on hold until the trial's conclusion. Her role was clear--to be a supportive wife. Yet the strain that came with that responsibility gnawed at her. The lack of control over the unfolding events spiked her anxiety to a higher level.

She trudged upstairs and peeked into Nate's room. He lay on his stomach, covers kicked off. Sitting beside him, she placed a hand on his back. Touching his tiny body provided her a moment of peace. He murmured a small, contented gurgle. Careful not to wake him, she whispered, "Your daddy's in trouble. He loves you, but has a lot on his mind."

Leaving his room, Jenny marveled at children's resilience. Problems seemed to slide off them like water. A setback barely slowed them; they simply moved on, smiles intact. Nate, thankfully, didn't share her worries. Most nights, he was asleep moments after his head touched the pillow.

Jenny climbed back into bed and forced herself to reflect on the positives: Nate's laughter, his boundless energy, and all the little things that made her proud. It was enough to help her relax. She pushed thoughts of Sam locked in his cold, damp cell from her mind. Tomorrow would bring plenty of time to think about him.

Chapter 39

GREGG HAD A ROUTINE for trial days—a ritual he relied on for focus and confidence. But today, that routine was disrupted. This trial was two hours north of his home, and instead of waking in his own bed, he awoke in a sterile hotel room, disoriented and mildly panicked. Sleep had been fitful, as it always was during trials. Like many trial lawyers, Gregg did what only they could understand-- staring at the ceiling at two in the morning, he practiced his opening statement over and over.

Most lawyers clung to a lucky suit—one they'd worn during a major win or an impactful appellate argument. Gregg didn't believe in lucky suits. Every one of his had borne witness to some courtroom disaster, either a client sentenced to prison or a judge tearing into his defense. For this trial, though, he decided to start fresh. He bought three new suits, planning to rotate them. None of these suits had yet to absorb failure. If Sam walked free, they'd become his new lucky charms.

At 7:00 a.m., he met Liz in the hotel lobby. They slammed down mediocre coffee and ate stale, semi-warm eggs. Had he been at home, he would have had his own homemade brew and a fresh bagel, but being up north prevented him from following his routine. They left fifteen minutes later to head to the courthouse. After a quick jaunt up the highway, they arrived, filled with nerves and attempting to boost each other's confidence. They walked up the immense metal doors just as the security guards began unlocking them and activating the metal detectors.

Liz pulled a dolly stacked with their two bulging document bags into the courtroom, while Gregg hauled their computers and A/V equipment. The setup would take nearly an hour, and Gregg wanted everything ready before the judge began jury selection at nine.

As they untangled wires behind the screen, Marcia McBride made her entrance. She, too, sported a new outfit, her usual confidence radiating. Trailing behind were Nguyen and Thompson, her novice associates, their nearly identical gray suits making them look like a matched set. Without a word, the two unloaded three document bags and began arranging their own A/V setup. Tapping at their laptops, they were ready to display evidence on the courtroom screens

While her minions organized their materials, McBride sidled up to Gregg. "Hey, you clean up well. I think the jurors are going to think you're hot, too."

Gregg didn't look up. "Thanks," he mumbled.

"No need to be huffy," she teased. "Just thought I'd say 'hi' while it's quiet." She leaned in closer. "And to let you know you smell nice. Some lawyers prep all night and forget to shower before court. That's bad manners, don't you think?"

Gregg glanced at her, his face blank. "Sure. Whatever you say."

Unbothered, she stepped back with a smile. "Well, good luck."

Gregg returned to sorting his papers.

At 8:57, the court's tipstaff peeked in. "Judge Denby will take the bench in three minutes. Jury selection will begin shortly."

The five lawyers took their seats—Gregg and Liz at one table, McBride at the other, with her two associates sitting behind her. Gregg turned to scan the room. In the back, Jenny sat beside a woman in her sixties wearing slacks and a sweater—Sam's mom. He gave them a quick wave. Closer to the front, six journalists sat with tablets at the ready. Gregg wondered how much coverage a small-town murder trial would get. Probably a lot, given the tawdry sex angle he anticipated the press would latch onto during testimony.

The tipstaff returned, commanding everyone to rise. Judge Denby entered, wasting no time. He directed deputies to bring in Sam, who was seated behind Gregg. Sam wore a new suit, courtesy of Jenny, looking surprisingly polished for someone who'd spent the past seven months in jail.

Next, the tipstaff brought in the jury venire—the 60 men and women summoned to serve. They filed into their assigned seats, arranged by identification numbers the court administrator had provided earlier.

Denby began with a concise summary of the case, informing the venire this was a murder trial. He clarified that under state law, this was not a capital case—if they found the defendant guilty, he would face a prison term, for which he would decide the duration, and there would be no consideration of the death penalty. The mention of murder and throwing out the concept of 'death penalty,' created buzz among the jurors, who sat a bit straighter in their seats realizing this was no petty theft matter they would be hearing, their curiosity and unease palpable.

For the next four hours, Denby and the attorneys questioned prospective jurors, probing for biases. None gave overt reasons for disqualification. At one point, Gregg leaned toward Liz and whispered, "If these people have biases against a criminal defendant, they're doing a great job hiding it."

The court provided demographic information on each juror, and the lawyers followed up with targeted questions, trying to gauge hidden prejudices. Despite their efforts, Gregg gleaned little insight into the jurors' motivations—a feeling he often had during jury selection.

Using their four peremptory challenges, Gregg and Liz removed those they believed were most likely to convict without fully considering reasonable doubt. When the process was complete, the final jury comprised seven men and five women, including two people of color. Gregg studied them as they took their seats but felt no closer to understanding how they might decide. He leaned toward Liz. "I'll tell you how well we did after the verdict."

Denby announced a ten-minute recess. "When we return, the prosecution will give its opening statement."

Gregg nodded at Sam and mouthed, "Let the festivities begin."

Chapter 40

E VERY PROSECUTOR HAS DIFFERENT motivation for wanting to put criminals behind bars. Some want to clean up the streets. Others believe convictions serve as deterrents to those who might consider committing a crime. For another group, it's the thrill of outmaneuvering defense attorneys who dare to represent guilty clients.

For Marcia McBride, her motivation today was singular—to win. Not because Sam Jordan might have committed the crime—that didn't matter to her—but because her career prospects hinged on a victory. A loss would relegate her to serving as District Attorney in this small town where domestic disputes were, most of the time, the most compelling cases her office handled. A win, however, would position her to seek her party's nomination for the U.S. Senate. For McBride, a conviction was the only acceptable outcome.

Having delivered hundreds of opening statements, McBride understood the power of a strong start. She believed that if she could strike the right chord, the jury would lean toward a conviction even before hearing from the defense. The prosecution's influence was immense, and if she could spark righteous indignation, her chances of getting a conviction would skyrocket.

As she approached the jury box, she remained silent, letting the weight of the moment settle over the courtroom. She locked eyes with each juror before finally speaking.

"On July 23rd of last year, the defendant, Samuel P. Jordan, entered the home of Pablo Marcon while Mr. Marcon was resting in bed. He placed a gun to his head and, in cold blood, shot him. The bullet obliterated his skull, splattering blood and brain matter across the wall and headboard."

At that moment, the three screens facing the jury illuminated, displaying two gruesome photographs of a man in his thirties, his lifeless body slumped in bed. The vivid red of blood mingled with gray brain matter creating a horrifying tableau.

The jury recoiled, just as McBride anticipated. She pressed on.

"Despite killing Mr. Marcon with the first shot, the defendant took aim again," now raising her hand and mimicking the motion of firing a gun. She continued, "This time, he fired a bullet into Mr. Marcon's chest, ripping his heart apart."

The jurors sat frozen, their wide eyes fixed on her. Satisfied, McBride lowered her hand, allowing them a moment to exhale a collective breath.

"How do we know the defendant is responsible for this murder?" she asked. "We don't have the gun that killed Mr. Marcon. There are no fingerprints tying Mr. Jordan to the crime scene, and of course, he has never confessed." She shrugged, as if to acknowledge the challenges of the case while suggesting compelling evidence would be forthcoming.

"But it's simple because we have three irrefutable pieces of evidence."

She held up one finger.

"First, Mr. Jordan lives two hours from the Marcon residence, yet his cell phone records and credit card transactions place him mere minutes from the crime scene at the exact time of the murder."

A second finger went up. "Second, his DNA was found in the house. You'll hear from one of the country's leading DNA experts, who will explain that the presence of his DNA confirms he was there. And Mr. Jordan had no legitimate reason to be in that home."

Finally, a third finger. "Third, although he never met Mr. Marcon, the defendant had a motive to kill him." She paused to let the gravity of her statement settle over the jurors before turning to gesture toward a woman seated nearby.

"This is Gina Marcon, Pablo's widow."

Gina, dressed in a somber black jacket and pants, nodded at the jurors, her gaze never meeting them.

"Years ago, Gina and the defendant worked together at a summer camp as counselors. Last year, Gina found him on social media and they reconnected. After exchanging messages, they met for dinner, but Mr. Jordan misread her intentions. He wanted a romantic relationship, but Gina rebuffed him and made it clear she was happily married. She eventually cut off contact. They exchanged a few more messages, but Gina made it clear that he had overstepped her boundaries and cut off contact.

"However, Mr. Jordan refused to accept this. He convinced himself that if Mr. Marcon was no longer in the picture, Gina would return his affections. In his delusion, he saw murder as the solution."

McBride's voice grew firmer, her cadence deliberate. She stood motionless before the jury. "He traveled to Gina's home, entered it, and, with two gunshots took away her husband and destroyed her life."

She paced slowly, letting her words linger.

"We are here because Sam Jordan couldn't accept reality. He clung to a fantasy where Gina Marcon would leave her husband for him. His obsession led him to commit an unthinkable crime."

Her tone intensified and her conviction remained unshakable. "After you hear the evidence, there will be no doubt in your minds. The only logical conclusion will be that Sam Jordan, beyond any reasonable doubt, murdered Pablo Marcon."

With her final words hanging in the air, McBride turned and returned to her seat, her pulse steadied as she settled in.

Chapter 41

G REGG PRESUMED EVERYONE HEARD his heart thumping as it pounded against his ribs. He had plenty of experience in front of juries, but never imagined he might get sick walking up to the jury box. Today, he felt an unfamiliar nausea rising. As he buttoned the top button of his suit, he prayed his trembling hands didn't betray the turmoil roiling inside him.

The jurors sat silent, waiting, allowing him space to draw a breath. "Ladies and gentlemen, while Pablo Marcon's murder is both despicable and tragic, Sam Jordan did not kill him. Sam stands before you an innocent man, unjustly accused of a crime because the prosecution rushed to judgment. They failed to un-cover the truth, to gather all the evidence, or even to preserve what evidence there was.

"You'll hear insinuations and suggestions about what might have happened that evening. But when you examine the facts closely, you'll see the pieces don't fit the story the prosecution is trying to sell.

"The State wants you to believe that Sam Jordan—a man who had never met or even seen Pablo Marcon—murdered him in cold blood and left incriminating DNA all over the scene. But when we look at the evidence, when you take the time to consider and examine it, it raises more questions than it answers. As jurors, your duty is to seek the truth by scrutinizing all the evidence. You must ask yourselves: Is there any reasonable doubt here? Has the prosecution truly proven their version of events?

"Let's start with the DNA evidence, the cornerstone of the prosecution's case. Yes, the lab reports indicate Sam's DNA was found in Pablo Marcon's bedroom. But DNA alone doesn't tell us how or when it got there. DNA can transfer easily and remain in a place for days—or even weeks. It does not prove Sam was there the night Pablo Marcon was killed. And it certainly doesn't prove he pulled the trigger. The prosecution won't tell you this because it creates reasonable doubt.

"They also don't want to tell you that although Mr. Jordan may have been close to the Marcon residence, there is zero evidence he ever was in it. They also want to hide from the fact that their own investigators may have been the ones who accidentally brought Sam's DNA onto the scene."

Gregg paused to scan the jurors. "You must examine every bit of the DNA evidence and ask yourself one simple question: Does it make sense or is it more likely they are trying to convict Sam on faulty evidence?"

"Then there's the missing murder weapon. The very object the prosecution claims Sam used to take Pablo Marcon's life, is nowhere to be found. You have to wonder if Sam meticulously planned this crime, would he be careless enough to leave DNA but somehow dispose of the murder weapon so completely that not a trace of it is found? It doesn't add up.

"And just as critical, Sam's fingerprints are nowhere at the scene. Not on the door, not on the bed frame, not on anything in Pablo Marcon's room. How could he commit this crime without leaving a single fingerprint? There's no sign of forced entry, no evidence that Sam ever set foot in that house and nothing to suggest he was present. The prosecution will attempt to explain this away, but the absence of fingerprints is a glaring problem they cannot resolve.

"At the end of this trial, we will ask you to do just one thing: Hold the State to its burden of proof. We don't have to prove Sam's innocence—our legal system requires the prosecution to prove his guilt beyond a reasonable doubt. Reasonable doubt means exactly that. If you have any reason to doubt the prosecution's story, you must find Sam Jordan not guilty. In this case, that doubt isn't just reasonable—it's undeniable."

Gregg paused, scanning the jurors one by one, then stepped back to his seat. He glanced at Sam, trying to gauge his reaction, but Sam's expression remained inscrutable.

Judge Denby addressed the courtroom. "It's been a long day. We'll begin testimony first thing in the morning. Please do not discuss the case amongst yourselves. Have a pleasant evening." With a nod to his tipstaff, the judge struck his gavel, and the jurors were escorted out.

Gregg placed a reassuring hand on Sam's shoulder. "I'll meet you here in the morning," he said in his ear.

Two court deputies arrived to escort Sam out. From across the room, Jenny and her mother waved goodbye to Gregg before slipping out through the back door.

Liz helped Gregg pack up the materials they needed for the evening's preparation into a document bag. "That went well, didn't it?" she asked, offering a small smile.

Gregg smirked, though his eyes held a shadow of uncertainty. "I'll let you know after the jury delivers its verdict."

Chapter 42

ONCE A TRIAL BEGINS, and the attorneys put on their game faces, they find it difficult to partake in normal, everyday small talk. Gregg was no different. Rather than engage with the prosecutors, he and Liz sat at counsel table, staring straight ahead. The morning light streamed in through the tall windows, but didn't lift their mood as Judge Denby called for the jury to be brought in.

"Call your first witness," Denby said, as if discussing the weather, once the jurors were in place.

Marcia McBride rose and turned toward the jury. "The Commonwealth calls Claire Temple."

Seated behind the prosecution, a young woman in her late thirties rose, clutching a brown folder against her chest. She approached the witness stand, the light scent of hotel soap trailing her, and waited in front of the bailiff, her right hand raised. This wasn't her first rodeo.

"Do you swear to tell the truth, so help you God?"

Temple wore a pair of grey slacks and a cream-colored blouse, both without a wrinkle, reflecting her professional and practical demeanor. Her auburn hair was pulled off her face, allowing an unobstructed view of her piercing green eyes. In a strong voice, she said, "I do," and took her seat in the witness box without awaiting further direction.

McBride took her place at the far edge of the jury box, hoping the jurors would focus on the witness's testimony. "Please tell the jury who you are."

"My name is Claire Temple. I am a crime scene investigator."

"What does a crime scene investigator do?"

"As the name suggests, I am responsible for investigating a crime scene. My team is called to a scene, where we document its appearance and direct the gathering of evidence. I ensure my team collects every relevant piece of evidence in a manner that doesn't compromise it. I also ensure the chain of custody is maintained until trial."

"Tell us about your experience as a crime scene investigator."

Temple shot a quick smile at the jurors. "I graduated from Boston University, Summa Cum Laude, fifteen years ago, with a bachelor's degree in criminal justice. I then did two paid internships in crime labs in Florida and North Carolina, where I learned how to investigate crimes and gather evidence at a crime scene."

"For the last twelve years, I've worked as an investigator with the County's Crime Investigation Unit. I've led investigations into over two hundred cases, and three years ago, I became the lead investigator. In this role, I also oversee and train eight other investigators."

"Do you keep up to date on the latest techniques in crime scene investigation?"

She nodded. "I do. I regularly attend continuing education classes in my field. Additionally, I've been teaching courses on the latest methodologies to undergraduates at the University of Pittsburgh, where I'm an adjunct professor in the field of criminology."

"Are you a member of any organizations or societies dedicated to educating students in these fields?"

"Yes. I am a Certified Crime Scene Investigator, or 'CCSI,' a certification granted by the International Association for Identification. I'm also an active member of the American Academy of Forensic Sciences, where I attend yearly conferences and contribute to peer-reviewed journals on crime scene reconstruction and evidence preservation."

McBride nodded and glanced at Gregg, who was jotting notes on his yellow pad. "Your Honor, the prosecution moves for the admission of Claire Temple as an expert crime scene investigator."

Denby turned his attention to Gregg. "Does the defense have any questions regarding this witness's qualifications?"

Gregg stood and walked toward Temple. He wasn't going to be able to do much damage here—picking apart her credentials would be pointless since her training in the field was more than sufficient. His goal was to start chipping away at her steely veneer.

"You've been a crime scene investigator for nearly fifteen years and have investigated many different crimes."

"That's correct."

"Can we agree that every crime scene is different?"

"Of course."

"And that you must be properly trained on how to handle evidence, or it's no good?"

"True."

"If you or anyone else working on a crime scene violates procedures, the evidence collected is unreliable. It's tainted."

"Yes, which is why training is so important." She spoke to the jurors, shifting the cadence of her voice to emphasize important concepts.

"And no matter what you learn in a classroom or continuing education course, following the appropriate procedures is paramount."

"I wouldn't put it that way, but we must adhere to proper procedures."

"You didn't train everyone who worked on this crime scene, did you?"

"I didn't."

"Then you can't offer testimony on whether they followed the proper procedures."

Before Temple could respond, McBride was on her feet. "Objection. Speculative. This question is irrelevant to her qualifications."

Denby considered the objection, but before he ruled, Gregg said, "I have no further questions at this time, but I will have more after the prosecution completes its direct examination."

Denby nodded at McBride. "Please continue with your direct examination."

McBride shook her head in frustration as the judge ignored her objection and Gregg's improper question hung in the air. She stepped forward. "Ms. Temple, were you involved in the investigation into the murder of Pablo Marcon?"

"I was."

"Please explain what you did."

Temple turned her body toward the jury ready to take charge and paint the picture of the crime scene for the jurors, who appeared wanting to listen. "There had been a 911 call by the victim's wife, reporting that her husband had been shot. Sergeant Caffey was the first officer on the scene. He secured the home and called for me and my team to document the evidence."

"What time was the 911 call?"

Temple glanced at her notes. "7:27 p.m."

"I'd like to play the call made by the victim's wife. Can you confirm that Exhibit 1 is a true and accurate recording of that call?"

"I can. It is the recording of the call she made."

Hearing no objection from the defense, Denby said, "You may play the recording."

McBride nodded at Jack Sanders, wearing yet another new suit, his hair slicked-back. He pushed a button on his computer, and the voice of the 911 operator crackled over the speakers for the jurors.

"This is 911. What is your emergency?"

Static hissed. Then, "This is 911. What is your emergency?"

In a high-pitched tone, Gina's voice rang out: "Oh my God. My husband. He's shot. He's bleeding."

"What is your name, ma'am?"

"Ah, Gina Marcon. Oh my God. It's horrible."

"Is he breathing?"

"I don't think so. There's so much blood."

"Are you safe where you are?"

"I don't know. I don't see anyone." Her voice quivered.

The 911 operator took Gina's address and assured her that police and paramedics would be sent immediately, keeping her on the line until the first responders arrived less than five minutes later, before terminating the call.

McBride looked over at the jury as the call played, noting that each juror focused intently on the words. Her confidence in them grew.

She addressed the witness. "Please tell us what you did when you arrived at the scene."

"My team is experienced in gathering evidence. By the time we arrived, the officers had secured the house and marked it as a crime scene. They directed me to the master bedroom on the second floor.

"Upon entering, we found a Hispanic male in his mid-thirties, already pronounced dead. He had a bullet wound to his right temple and an exit wound on the left side of his head. There was also a bullet wound to the chest, likely a shot directly to the heart. Blood was splattered on the sheets, pillows, and wall behind him. Skull fragments and brain matter were mixed with the blood."

"So, what did your team do next?"

"The first thing I did was to make entries in my log. I log the time of our arrival. I document every step of our investigation, noting each piece of evidence we collect."

McBride grabbed a manila folder from Sanders and snatched a set of papers from it. She handed copies to Gregg and the court reporter. "I'm marking as Exhibit 2 a document. Will you please identify this for the jurors."

Temple scanned the document. "This is my crime log. It details the time of arrival and the time we completed our investigation. It also includes my notes on what our investigation entailed."

McBride nodded. "What did you do next?"

"One of my investigators took photographs of the scene to memorialize everything from the position of the body to the location of the blood and any other significant details. He also took other shots in and outside the house, but none were relevant to my investigation."

As Temple completed her thought, McBride handed her a set of photographs. "Are these the pictures taken that night?"

Temple flipped through them. "They are."

"Do they accurately depict the scene?"

"They do. They show the location of everything we found in the room."

"Your Honor, may we publish these, marked as Exhibit 3, to the jury?"

The Judge glanced at Gregg, who responded, "Your Honor, these are subject to your prior ruling regarding certain photos of the decedent."

"We've removed those photographs from the exhibit, consistent with your prior ruling," McBride said, as if discussing paint colors rather than gruesome images showing portions of Pablo Marcon's head blown off the judge had ruled inadmissible.

"You may show the jurors Exhibit 3."

For the next ten minutes, the jurors passed the photographs from juror number one to juror number twelve. Silence prevailed, and only a couple of the jurors recoiled in any sort of a demonstrable manner while viewing the images of Pablo, dead on his bloody sheets.

McBride wanted to emphasize the gory nature of the murder. "Ms. Temple, can you please describe how the victim was found that evening?"

A block of four photographs appeared on the screen, each showing a different view of Pablo Marcon in bed after being shot. Temple leaned forward as the jurors did the same. "These pictures show how Mr. Marcon was found in bed at the time he was shot. I found no evidence his body had been moved. Blood saturated his pillow." She used a laser pointer to highlight specific areas of the photos. "The chest wound caused blood to pool on the bed, with blood splatter behind the victim. We also confirmed that pieces of his brain were lodged against the wall, mixed in with his blood."

Three jurors turned away from the screen and closed their eyes. McBride paused to give them a moment to recover.

"What else did you do during your investigation?"

"I conducted a preliminary examination of the body, checking for blood, hair, body position, and signs of trauma. I noted the bullet wounds. The pathologist would perform a more detailed examination after the body was moved to the morgue."

"Did you collect blood samples?"

"Yes. We collected blood samples from all locations where we found it. This included from the deceased, the bed, the floor, and the walls."

"Did you gather DNA samples?"

"Yes. We took samples for DNA testing, including blood, hair, and skin samples. We also gathered material from the deceased including getting samples from under his fingertips and from his mouth. The labs we use are responsible for the testing."

"Anything else?"

"We dusted for fingerprints."

"What did you find?"

"The only prints we found in the bedroom were those of the deceased and his wife. We found no other unidentified prints in the house that we couldn't eliminate, meaning they belonged to identified friends, relatives, and the cleaner."

"Anything further?"

"We looked for weapons but found none. We searched the entire house, yard, and surrounding neighborhood."

"How about ballistic samples?"

"We found two sets of bullet fragments. One in the deceased's bed, which passed through his chest; the other entered his head and then lodged in the headboard. We gathered the fragments and sent them for ballistics examination."

"How long did this process take?"

"We were on scene for about six hours. We conducted our initial walkthrough and then repeated the process to ensure we didn't overlook anything. Once we were done, I released the scene back to the principal officer in charge."

"Did you find anything unusual?"

"Not really. I've seen many scenes like this. You sometimes find fingerprints. There's always blood and, therefore, DNA. We take pictures. The fact that the gun was never found is not unusual. Murderers often don't leave their weapons behind."

"Thank you, Ms. Temple. Defense counsel may have a few questions for you."

Judge Denby spoke. "Let's take our morning break. Counsel can cross-examine the witness when we return."

Gregg leaned into Liz. "Let's talk in the hall to make sure we have everything we need for cross." She gathered some papers and grabbed her yellow pad, allowing Gregg to lead her out the door.

Chapter 43

THE HALLWAY OUTSIDE THE courtroom was narrow, so Liz and Gregg walked toward the open rotunda. They stood in the light streaming down from the stained-glass roof. The smell of coffee wafted up to them from the throngs of people waiting in the hallways of the floors below. Gregg flipped through some notes and said, "The investigator sets the scene but doesn't score too many points. The key witnesses come later. What's our strategy here?"

Liz smiled, knowing the answer. "Hit the witness a couple of times. Get out without doing any damage to our case. Basically, don't let her repeat her story, yet create doubt for the jury."

Gregg nodded. "Exactly. We need to plant a little doubt with each witness and hope it raises questions in the jurors' minds that the prosecution can't answer." He grinned. "And don't say, 'basically.' It adds nothing."

"I think you're good with her." As Liz finished her statement, Marcia McBride sauntered over and touched Gregg on the arm. "The judge wants to start, sweetie. Can't wait to watch you shake your butt while questioning my witness."

She winked and walked away. Damn, this woman is way too cocky, Gregg thought, as he and Liz followed her back into the courtroom.

After a few minutes, the judge returned. He instructed the bailiff to bring in the jury and motioned for the witness to return to the stand. Once the jurors were seated, the judge nodded at Gregg. "You may cross-examine."

Gregg moved to the far side of the room, away from the jury box, deliberately placing himself where the witness couldn't easily turn to the jurors. "Ma'am, let me follow up on some points you raised during your direct examination. You indicated that you and your team dusted for fingerprints."

"That's correct."

"You checked the entire house for prints."

"Yes."

"Every room?"

"Yes."

"You also dusted outside the house?"

"Correct." Temple attempted to direct her testimony to the jurors, but this only caused her head to swing like a pendulum.

"Despite your best efforts, you didn't find Mr. Jordan's fingerprints anywhere on the crime scene, did you?"

"We didn't."

"You didn't find any fingerprint of Mr. Jordan within miles of the house, did you?"

"No, we didn't."

Gregg shifted forward. "You said you found the fingerprints of other people in the house."

"True. People who were expected to be there."

"Like Mrs. Marcon and her housekeeper?"

"Correct."

"Could they have killed Mr. Marcon?"

"Objection," McBride interjected, standing. "Speculation."

"Overruled," the judge said. "The witness will answer."

Temple turned her attention back to Gregg. "There's no evidence anyone other than the defendant killed Mr. Marcon."

Gregg noted that the witness's tone and demeanor remained unchanged from her direct examination. Like most of the prosecution's witnesses, she was a seasoned professional, determined not to give the impression that her investigation was anything but objective.

"Did you ever consider anyone other than Mr. Jordan as a suspect?"

"It's not my job to determine who the suspects are. That's the detective's responsibility. But my understanding is that once the DNA evidence came back, no one else was considered a suspect."

Gregg didn't flinch despite the urge to jerk his entire body. "Since you had nothing to do with reviewing the DNA evidence, let's hold off on discussing it until we have a witness who can speak to that. Is that okay?"

"Sure."

Having the witness admit she didn't have DNA expertise emboldened Gregg for a moment.

"Because you don't know any more about interpreting DNA evidence than anyone else."

The witness hesitated briefly, then responded, "I guess."

Gregg grinned and switched topics. "You indicated that no weapon was found at the scene."

"That's correct."

"And despite your best efforts, you never found one."

"Correct."

"Anywhere, or at any time?"

"Also correct."

"Which means no prosecution witness can testify about the gun that killed Mr. Marcon."

"I guess that's true."

"Nobody can say where the gun came from, who owned it, or what happened to it."

"Also true."

The point with the gun being nailed down, Gregg moved his questioning in another direction. "Finally, Ms. Temple, according to your log notes from the evening, your initial suspicion was that this was a burglary gone wrong. True?"

"That is true, although we moved away from that theory quickly."

"Not quick enough that you let the theory leak to the newspapers."

"I'm not sure how the reporters got the information, but, yes, some outlets reported that this started as a botched robbery."

Gregg smirked. "Thank you. Now, let's look at your log." He nodded to Liz, who tapped on her computer. The report appeared on the screens in the courtroom. "Let me read from the highlighted section, and you tell me if I read it accurately: 'The bedroom was in disarray, as were other rooms in the house. I presumed this was a burglary, but the burglar was surprised to find the deceased in bed so early in the evening.' Did I read that accurately?"

"You did."

"So, correct me if I'm wrong. Based on your investigation that night, including an inspection of the entire house, you believed the crime began as a burglary and that Mr. Marcon was killed when the burglar found him asleep in bed?"

"That was my initial supposition."

"One which was supported by the evidence."

"Initially, perhaps. But we later learned that this was the usual state of the house."

"Perhaps," Gregg interjected, "but it was early in the evening. Nobody would expect to find someone in bed at that time. So, your theory that this was a burglary gone wrong aligns with what you found that night."

"Perhaps, but after a more thorough review of the evidence, the theory was no longer supported."

"And you would agree the police later searched Mr. Jordan's home, didn't they?"

"They did."

"And you'll agree the police found nothing at his house to support your theory that this started as a burglary?"

"That's true."

"Nothing to indicate Mr. Jordan was a burglar, and nothing stolen from the Marcon residence, correct?"

"That is also correct."

"And despite never finding Mr. Jordan's fingerprints anywhere and never locating the murder weapon, the detective concluded that Mr. Jordan was the killer."

"Yes, and with good reason."

"I have no further questions for this witness." Gregg returned to his counsel table and found a note Liz had placed in front of his seat: 'I think you uncovered some reasonable doubt in your cross.' He turned to Liz and offered a quick smile.

McBride rose from her chair. "I have a brief redirect, Your Honor." The judge nodded.

"Ms. Temple, with regard to noting that this was a possible burglary, could you explain your thought process and why you ruled it out?"

"Of course. I often theorize at the start of an investigation based on an initial inspection, but that's never a final conclusion. I remain open to new evidence and want to ensure any suppositions I make align with the facts."

She glanced at the ceiling before returning her gaze to the jurors. "Although I considered the break-in angle, a more thorough review of the evidence showed this wasn't a burglary. There was no sign of forced entry, and no unlocked doors. I spoke with Mrs. Marcon, who informed me that their house was often in disarray, and the condition I found the house in was exactly how she had left it when she went to the mall. After reviewing the contents of the home, she confirmed nothing had been taken—nothing had been moved. As our investigation progressed, it became clear this wasn't a burglary. It was a murder."

"Thank you. I have no further questions."

Gregg stood. "Nothing more, Your Honor."

Denby looked at the witness. "You're dismissed."

Temple walked off the stand and out of the courtroom. Sam turned to Liz and whispered, "One witness down. Maybe a bit of doubt created. Let's brace for the next one."

Chapter 44

JUDGE DENBY HAD A reputation for moving his trials with little delay. Even after just one witness, he gave no indication that he would allow the jury to twiddle its collective thumbs. Without looking up, he said, "Call your next witness."

McBride stood. "The prosecution calls Dr. Leonard Graham."

A squat man in his early fifties, with salt-and-pepper hair and a bushy mustache, giving him a passing resemblance to a walrus, rose from the gallery. The doctor walked with deliberate steps past Sam, sitting behind counsel table expressionless, and approached the witness stand. He paid no one on the defense team any heed, and after swearing his oath to tell the truth, took his seat. He pulled his shoulders back, giving himself a greater air of authority. Gregg realized again that this was an experienced witness who would be comfortable with the back-and-forth of cross-examination.

"Please state your name and occupation," McBride commanded.

"My name is Leonard Graham. I am Elk County's Chief Medical Examiner."

"Will you please outline your medical training and experience for the jury."

"Of course. I have a medical degree from the University of Pittsburgh School of Medicine, with a specialty in forensic pathology. After completing my residency at Citizens General Hospital, I joined the Medical Examiner's Office in Las Vegas, where I worked for ten years. For the past twelve years, I have served as the Chief Medical Examiner here in Elk County. In my career, I have performed over five thousand autopsies and have testified in numerous trials as an expert witness in forensic pathology."

McBride turned towards the judge. "The people offer Dr. Graham as an expert in the field of Medical Pathology."

"Any objections?"

Gregg half-stood. "None, Your Honor."

Denby glanced back at the prosecutor. "You may proceed."

"Dr. Graham, would you please describe your involvement in this case?"

As McBride finished her question, the doctor turned his attention to the jurors and addressed them. "On the night of July 23rd, I was called to the scene of a homicide at 414 Roundcliff Road. I conducted a preliminary examination of the deceased at the scene and later performed a full autopsy at the county morgue."

"Who was the deceased?"

"The deceased was identified as Pablo Marcon, a thirty-five-year-old male, who, when I arrived, had been shot in his head and chest, and lay dead in his bed."

"Dr. Graham, please summarize your findings from the autopsy?"

"Yes. Mr. Marcon sustained two gunshot wounds: one to his head and the other to his chest, through his heart. The first bullet, the one that killed him, entered the right temple and exited through the left side of the skull, causing extensive damage to the brain. Based on the characteristics of the wound, I determined that the shot was fired at close range, likely within a few inches. This shot would have immediately killed him.

"The second shot was superfluous. It entered his chest, passing through his right ventricle and exiting near his left shoulder. The second wound likely would have been sufficient to kill Mr. Marcon, but, as I mentioned, the first bullet already had done its damage."

McBride moved to the prosecution's table and retrieved a series of photographs, which she handed to the bailiff, who gave them to the witness. "Doctor, I've shown you what we have marked as Prosecution Exhibit 4. Can you identify these photographs?"

Graham took his time leafing through the photos. "These are pictures of the deceased in bed, his position at the time of death. They demonstrate he was in a reclined position when shot. The second set is a series of pictures taken of the exit wounds during the autopsy. They show the direction of the exit wound."

McBride delayed for a few moments to allow the jurors time to review the photographs now being displayed on the monitors.

"What conclusions can you draw from your examination at the autopsy?"

Graham shifted his body towards the jurors. "First, the gun was fired at close range. There are several indicators of this, including the presence of gunpowder stippling, which are tiny burns and particles embedded in the skin surrounding the entry wound. This stippling is characteristic of a shot fired from six inches or less. In addition, the pattern of soot deposition around both wounds indicates the muzzle of the firearm was in close proximity to Mr. Marcon when it was discharged."

"Did you also find any foreign material or residue on the deceased?"

Graham nodded. "We checked the body for strands of hair or other foreign matter—anything that might contain DNA. We found a few strands of hair which I sent to the lab for testing. Those belonged to the victim's wife. I also scraped under the victim's nails. Most times, we find something under the nails. I sent that material to the lab for additional testing."

"Did the lab find any relevance to the materials found under Mr. Marcon's fingernails?"

"Yes, it did." Graham paused to gather his thoughts. "The material under his fingernails included small bits of blood and DNA that matched the defendant, Samuel Jordan."

A hush enveloped the courtroom. Sam's mother grabbed Jenny's arm and squeezed. Jenny forced herself not to react.

McBride continued, "Based on your findings, can you estimate the time of death?"

"Given the body's temperature, the extent of *rigor mortis*, and other factors I use in these situations, I estimated that Mr. Marcon died between 6 p.m. and 7 p.m. on July 23rd of last year."

"Doctor, are the opinions you offer today given within a reasonable degree of scientific certainty?"

"They are. I have no doubt Mr. Marcon died as a result of a bullet wound delivered at close range."

"Thank you, Doctor. Please remain seated in case counsel for the defense has any questions," McBride said, as if the doctor didn't understand he was still subject to cross-examination.

Gregg walked to the far side of the courtroom. He introduced himself to the doctor and asked, "Doctor, you said the gunshot that killed Mr. Marcon was delivered at close range, correct?"

"I said that, yes."

"Extremely close range. Like a matter of inches."

"Correct."

"Could you tell from your autopsy whether Mr. Marcon was asleep at the time this happened?"

"Not with any degree of certainty. Given the time he was shot and that he was wearing shorts and a T-shirt, it was likely he was relaxing. His wife indicated he wasn't feeling well, so perhaps he had dozed off. The oxygen saturation levels at the time of death, however, don't conclusively establish whether he was asleep."

"Thank you, Doctor. So let me see if I understand. We have a situation with no forced entry into the house."

"I am unaware of any evidence of such."

"Nothing was taken from the house, and Mr. Marcon is shot at close range in his bed."

"That is correct."

"You found no sign of struggle."

"Well, he was shot."

Gregg gave a half-hearted smile. "Doctor, often in situations like this, if an unknown person entered Mr. Marcon's bedroom, he would expect Mr. Marcon to protect himself."

"Perhaps."

"And if he made such an attempt, a violent struggle might ensue."

"You're speculating, but it's a possibility."

"And if a violent struggle ensued, then Mr. Marcon's body would show evidence of the struggle. This would include bruising, scrapes, and cuts. Right?"

"That might happen."

"Yet, and you would agree with this, you found no evidence of a struggle, did you?"

"Other than the skin and DNA materials found under Mr. Marcon's nails, I did not find any."

"No bruising?"

"None, other than from the bullet wounds."

"No cuts?"

"Correct."

"And no broken bones?"

"Also correct."

"In fact, you found Mr. Marcon lying in bed as if he hadn't moved a muscle."

"I guess that's true." Graham shifted his weight away from Gregg.

"So, we have a person who enters his bedroom. Mr. Marcon is in bed. The sun hasn't set, so light still enters the room. It doesn't appear as if he's asleep. And yet, this person can walk up to his bed, put a gun to his head, and shoot him without the deceased moving a muscle or attempting to stop this person?"

"I wasn't there, so I can't say with precision what happened. What I can offer is that Mr. Marcon was killed by a bullet shot at close range while he lay in his bed."

Gregg put on his best 'I'm perplexed' face. "Come on, Doctor, you're not expecting this jury to believe that some stranger, a person unknown to Mr. Marcon, was able to walk into his bedroom and pull out a gun without Mr. Marcon reacting in any way?"

The doctor shook his head. "I'm not saying anything to this jury other than what I found, which was that he died from a bullet fired at close range."

"Thank you, Doctor. I have no further questions."

As the witness gathered his materials and left the stand, Judge Denby glanced at the clock in the back of the courtroom. "Let's end the day here. We will resume testimony first thing tomorrow morning." He motioned to his tipstaff, who directed the jurors to exit in single file through the door at the front of the room.

Gregg walked over to Sam, whose face was still expressionless, and said, "That went as well as possible. We're just trying to poke some holes in their case at this point."

"I understand," Sam said. "This is brutal, having to listen to this crap. Are the jurors buying any of it?"

"I can't tell. Just remember, we only need one to find you not guilty. There's a lot of doubt I hope to pile up by the end of this trial."

Liz walked over and patted Sam on the arm. "He's the best," she said, pointing at Gregg.

"I know. My life's in his hands."

The guard who had been seated behind Sam the whole day rose and nodded at Gregg, who said, "We're ready. You can take him."

The guard pulled out his cuffs, placed them on Sam, and led him out of the courtroom.

Liz shook her head. "This is rough. He has to listen to this testimony all day without reacting, and then they take him back and lock him up at night."

"This is nothing compared to rotting in prison for the next thirty years, which is what he's facing if we can't convince someone on this jury to disagree with the prosecution."

"I know. That's why I'm going back to the hotel and organizing all our evidence for tomorrow."

They walked out of the courtroom together without saying another word.

Chapter 45

I T WAS ONLY THE second full day of testimony, yet the stress was already taking its toll on Gregg. He knew the prosecution's plan, and he was getting exactly what he expected—a steady, unrelenting stream of witnesses who, when taken together, would paint a compelling picture of Sam's involvement in the murder. He still didn't want to believe Sam might have been involved in what had happened to Pablo Marcon, but whether he believed it didn't matter. The only thing that mattered was what the jurors were thinking. At this point, he could only imagine the impact the onslaught was having on their minds.

Had he created any doubt with the jury? Or were they like lemmings, following the prosecution's lead and willing to convict Sam regardless of the evidence? Not knowing the answer until they rendered their verdict was gut wrenching in any case. Here he was defending his best friend, and his insides were in a constant state of turmoil. It wouldn't get any better until the trial was over.

Today would bring more expert testimony, as the prosecution continued its relentless parade of what Gregg believed were their theories disguised as facts, all presented through their witnesses.

When Marcia McBride announced they would be calling Evelyn Scott, Gregg didn't react. He had his cross-examination outline ready. The petite woman, in her early forties, took the stand. The round glasses perched on her nose, combined with the bangs hanging down her forehead, gave her the look of someone more comfortable with accounting than firearms. But when she listed her qualifications, everyone understood she knew her stuff when it came to guns.

She rattled off her education, which included a Ph.D. in Forensic Science, and her experience as a lead ballistics analyst for the FBI for ten years. Like all of the prosecution's experts, she recited her experience testifying in court, and Gregg assumed the jury saw it as a measure of competence, not, as he hoped, a sign that she might be for sale.

Bottom line, the ballistics analysis wasn't the most important aspect of the case. No one disputed that two bullets had been fired that night—a kill shot to the head, and another, just for good measure, to the chest. The bullets had come from the same gun, but, like everyone else, this expert had no idea what weapon was used to fire the shots, nor what had happened to it after the murder.

Dr. Scott confirmed that the shape of the bullet fragments indicated the shots had been fired from close range, but on cross-examination conceded that she believed Sam was the shooter solely because he was the only suspect the police had investigated. She had nothing additional to point at to conclude Sam had pulled the trigger. Gregg's questioning of the witness didn't last long.

He made his points, emphasizing that this witness offered little to advance the prosecution's case. He sensed the jury's impatience, eager for more definitive evidence of the shooter's identity. He knew the prosecution's list of witnesses for the day, and recognized they wouldn't have to wait much longer for that evidence.

Scott was off the stand and out of the courtroom after less than two hours of testimony. Gregg hadn't done anything significant to cast doubt on the prosecution's case with his questioning, but he hadn't expected to. The good news, he thought, was that she hadn't delivered any devastating blows. She had only added a few more bricks to the unyielding wall McBride was building for the jurors.

The next witness, who waited with a small smirk on his face in the back of the courtroom, clutching his little notebook like it was the nuclear football, would likely be the one to add the mortar that would seal the bricks forming the barrier slowly trapping Sam. Gregg's mind was already working on ways to prevent the witness from accomplishing his objective.

As the ballistics expert walked out of the courtroom, Denby announced they would take an early lunch so he could attend a meeting. He ordered everyone to return and be ready to present more testimony in two hours. Gregg thought, it's good to be the boss.

Chapter 46

S AM SLUMPED IN HIS chair, staring at the ceiling. The guards had just returned him from the holding cell, the place he'd spent his lunch break—handcuffed and left alone with a sandwich. For nearly one hundred twenty minutes, his only company had been his thoughts, replaying over and over his relationship with Gina, from the moment they met at camp to the one dinner they shared.

Back in the courtroom now, he couldn't shut off his mind. Gregg had told him the prosecution would call their DNA expert next, and they both understood that everything so far had only been a prelude to this witness. His testimony would be a crucial link in the prosecution's effort to prove Sam's guilt.

Spectators were returning to their seats as the bailiff ushered in the jurors, their collective gaze locked on their chairs. They hadn't made eye contact with anyone on either side since the trial began. Sam hoped for a supportive glance from at least one juror each time they entered, but so far, he'd received nothing—not a look, a peep or even a glimpse in his direction. He sank into his seat, bracing for the coming storm.

Judge Denby again nodded in Marcia McBride's direction, signaling for her to proceed. She rose and announced, "The prosecution calls Doctor Alan Whitmore."

Sam turned and this time spied another fifty-something year old man in a suit and a vest rise. His salt-and-pepper hair combed over his ears. The laugh lines around his eyes gave him the appearance of an amiable, country doctor—not the hired assassin Sam knew him to be.

After taking the stand, Whitmore introduced himself as a Ph.D. Molecular Biologist with training from Stanford. He had worked in forensic DNA analysis for over thirty years and was now the director of the Genetics Laboratory at the National Institute of Criminology, overseeing DNA analysis in criminal investigations. McBride took her time walking him through his credentials, carefully highlighting his publications in a journal he described as "the most reputable, peer-reviewed publication in forensic DNA analysis."

She then guided him through his faculty positions and the courses he taught at Pepperdine University, emphasizing how he was responsible for training the next generation of DNA experts. She also casually mentioned the awards he had won for teaching excellence. Whitmore made no attempt to boast about his accomplishments, but McBride skillfully gave the impression that she was coaxing the information from him in a modest manner with questions like, "Doctor, please give us a little more detail about the awards you have won," or "I've read your resume, please tell the jury about how your peers view your accomplishments."

During Gregg's questioning, it was clear that, despite his attempts to challenge the witness's qualifications, this expert was as legitimate as they came—even more so than the previous witnesses. Everyone knew Whitmore was a leading authority in the field of DNA analysis.

The witness shifted his attention to McBride as Gregg finished his questions on qualifications.

Sam slumped a little deeper in his chair, his heart pounding.

McBride didn't waste any time getting to the meat of the witness's substantive testimony. "Doctor, would you please explain to the jury what DNA is and how it is used in criminal investigations?"

Whitmore leaned forward, addressing the jurors with a teacher's calm demeanor. "Of course. DNA, or deoxyribonucleic acid, is the hereditary material in humans and nearly all other organisms. It's found in every cell of our bodies and carries the genetic instructions needed for growth, development, functioning, and reproduction of everything living."

Understanding that most jurors' knowledge of DNA was limited to TV crime dramas, he paused to let the information sink in before continuing. "Each person's DNA is unique, except in the case of identical twins. This uniqueness makes DNA a powerful tool in identifying individuals. In criminal investigations, we use DNA to link a suspect to a crime scene or to a victim through what we call 'biological evidence.'"

Whitmore picked up a pointer and directed the jury's attention to a screen displaying an image of a double helix. "This is a representation of the DNA molecule. It's structured like a twisted ladder, with pairs of molecules called nucleotides forming the rungs. These nucleotides are organized into sequences that code for the proteins in our body, making each person's DNA distinct."

He clicked to the next slide, showing a diagram of a cell. "DNA is located in the nucleus of our cells. In forensic investigations, we can extract DNA from biological materials found at a crime scene—such as blood, skin cells, hair, saliva, or even bone."

Dr. Whitmore then displayed an image illustrating DNA extraction. "Once we have a sample, we extract the DNA and amplify it using a technique called Polymerase Chain Reaction, or PCR. This allows us to create millions of copies of specific DNA segments, which can then be analyzed in detail."

The next slide displayed a graph illustrating DNA profiles. "One common method of DNA analysis in forensic science is Short Tandem Repeat (STR) analysis. STRs are short sequences of DNA that repeat in specific regions of the genome. The number of repeats varies among individuals. By examining these patterns, we can create a unique DNA profile."

McBride interjected, "Dr. Whitmore, please explain how these DNA profiles are compared in a criminal investigation?"

"My pleasure," Whitmore replied. "In a criminal investigation, the DNA profile from the crime scene sample is compared to the DNA profile of a suspect. If the profiles match, it strongly suggests the suspect was present at the crime scene or encountered the victim. The more markers that match, the higher the probability that the DNA belongs to the suspect."

He clicked to the next slide, showing a bar graph with statistical probabilities. "We also calculate the likelihood the DNA belongs to someone else. For example, in this case, the probability of the DNA found at the scene belonging to someone other than Mr. Jordan is less than one in a billion."

Sam glared at the jurors, disgusted. They were lapping up every word the witness was telling them, privileged to learn at the feet of a master.

McBride shifted the focus. "Now, Doctor, please tell us about the DNA evidence you analyzed in this case and the conclusions you were able to draw?"

The next slide appeared, and Whitmore turned his attention to it. The jurors followed his lead as the image displayed a picture of the crime scene. "This is the victim's position when investigators gathered samples for DNA evaluation. They collected blood samples from the bed sheets and the wall behind the victim." He pointed to these areas with a laser dot, guiding the jurors.

"What other DNA samples were collected?"

"It's standard procedure to examine the body and collect samples, including hair, skin, and even nasal swabs, as well as material from under the victim's fingernails."

"Why is it important to take samples from under the victim's fingernails?"

"In such cases, there's often some contact between the victim and the killer, It can be in the form of a struggle or even brief contact."

"Here, we've heard there were no signs of an overt struggle. Would this affect your conclusions?"

"No, it wouldn't. Even without an obvious struggle, the victim might have reached out to protect himself. A small amount of contact with the assailant can result in microscopic transfer of skin particles and therefore DNA, from the shooter to the victim."

McBride pressed further. "Does finding DNA under Mr. Marcon's fingernails prove that person was the killer?"

Whitmore shook his head. "No, it doesn't. It simply means that person had recent contact with the victim. We found his wife's DNA under his fingernails. This is not surprising. What would raise suspicion and merit further investigation is finding the DNA of someone who shouldn't have had contact with the victim. That's part of the puzzle we're putting together."

"So, what did your analysis of the DNA samples from the murder scene reveal?"

"First, we obtained Mr. Jordan's DNA sample, which was then analyzed using PCR and STR methods. The DNA extracted from the crime scene samples, including blood and skin cells, was compared to Mr. Jordan's. Both the blood samples and the skin material taken from underneath the victim's fingernails matched."

Another diagram appeared on the screen. "You can see from this chart that the crime scene samples were an exact match to Mr. Jordan's DNA." He pointed at the diagram and then turned to the jurors to gage their reaction.

"Doctor, you've explained how DNA is used in criminal investigations. Could you now explain how you determined the probability that the DNA from the crime scene and Mr. Jordan's DNA are a match?"

Whitmore nodded. "We analyze DNA by examining specific regions called Short Tandem Repeats, or STRs. These short sequences repeat in unique patterns. The number of repeats varies greatly among individuals, making STRs highly effective for creating individual DNA profiles."

He pointed to a slide on the screen showing a DNA profile chart. "A typical forensic DNA profile looks at multiple STR loci, or locations, across the genome. Each STR locus is like a unique marker that can distinguish one individual from another. For example, one person might have five repeats of a sequence at a particular locus, while another might have seven. By comparing these patterns at multiple locations across the genome, we create a profile specific to that person."

He pointed to the next slide, displaying DNA profiles side by side. "In this case, we examined twenty STR loci. The DNA profiles from the crime scene—both blood and skin—matched Mr. Jordan's at all twenty loci."

Turning back to the jury, he explained, "To determine the probability of a coincidental match, we use population databases, which contain information on STR patterns in different populations. By calculating the frequencies of these matches, we can determine how likely it is for someone other than Mr. Jordan to have the same DNA profile."

Whitmore pointed to another chart displaying the probability calculation. "In this case, the probability of someone other than

Mr. Jordan having the same DNA profile is for statistical purposes, less than one in a billion. In other words, it's effectively zero."

He paused, letting the weight of the evidence sink in. "To put it in simple terms, when we say the DNA profile from the crime scene matches Mr. Jordan's profile, we mean that the patterns at all the tested loci are identical. The probability of this match occurring by chance is so small that it provides overwhelming evidence that the DNA at the scene belongs to Mr. Jordan."

"Dr. Whitmore, are you offering any opinions about what happened at the crime scene or who killed Mr. Marcon?"

"I'm not. My only conclusion is that the DNA found at the crime scene—both the blood and the DNA under the victim's fingernails—matches Mr. Jordan's." He held up his hand. "Beyond that, I'm not offering any other conclusions."

"Thank you, Doctor. No further questions."

Denby turned to Gregg. "Counsel, would you like a recess before your cross-examination?"

Gregg stood. "Yes, Your Honor."

Denby dismissed the jurors with instructions to return in twenty minutes.

Sam stood and bowed his head, not even attempting to catch a juror's glance, knowing none would be forthcoming.

Chapter 47

T HE COURT GRANTED GREGG permission to take Sam into the hallway. Though a guard shadowed them wherever they went, Sam and his two lawyers managed to find a corner secluded enough for a private discussion.

Gregg grabbed Sam's arm, his voice sharp but low. "Your hair's a mess. Fix it."

Sam quickly ran his hand over his head, smoothing the wayward strands back into place.

"You can't let the jury think any testimony has gotten to you," Gregg insisted.

"I know. I know," Sam muttered, shaking his head. "But they're saying my DNA was at the scene. How the fuck does that happen?"

Gregg tightened his grip on Sam's shoulder, steadying him. "We saw their report. This isn't a surprise. You have to act like you expected this."

"Every time I hear it, it feels like a punch to the gut. I'm dying inside," Sam confessed.

Liz stepped forward and placed a hand on Sam's shoulder. "We've got this under control. We have a plan."

Sam spun away, frustration radiating from him. "That's a load of crap. You've given me no reason to believe you have it under control. Don't lie to me." He turned back abruptly, his glare piercing Liz. "This is my life." He paused, trying to calm himself. "That DNA wasn't mine. Figure it out."

Without waiting for a response, Sam turned and strode toward the courtroom. Gregg, Liz, and the guard followed silently.

Gregg stood before the witness, a calculated silence stretching between them. He knew the fate of his friend hinged on this cross-examination and his ability to undermine the witness's unrelenting confidence and poke holes in his conclusions.

"Dr. Whitmore," Gregg began, attempting to avoid the sound of overt sarcasm, "thank you for your detailed explanation of DNA profiling. I'd like to revisit some aspects of your testimony."

"Of course," Whitmore replied in the same detached manner he had used to reply to McBride's questions.

Gregg leaned forward on the podium, adopting a conversational posture. "You mentioned that the probability of a match between the DNA from the crime scene and Mr. Jordan's DNA was less than one in a billion. That's a staggering statistic, isn't it?"

"Yes, it's a very powerful indicator of a match," Whitmore confirmed.

Gregg nodded, as though agreeing. "And this probability is based on comparisons between the crime scene DNA profile and population database profiles, correct?"

"Correct," Whitmore affirmed. "We use databases to determine the frequency of specific STR patterns and calculate the likelihood of a coincidental match."

Gregg's expression grew more serious. "How comprehensive are these databases? Do they account for the full genetic diversity across all populations?"

"The databases are representative of various populations and are updated regularly to reflect new data," Whitmore explained. "They include samples from diverse ethnic and geographic groups."

Gregg pressed on. "But these databases have limitations, don't they? If certain populations are underrepresented, wouldn't that skew the probability calculations?"

Whitmore hesitated for a moment. "While it's true that no database can encompass every genetic variation, the ones we use are statistically robust and reliable for forensic purposes. The likelihood of significant deviation is extremely remote."

Gregg seized the opening. "So, there's a margin for error. And if a group with similar genetics to Mr. Jordan is underrepresented in your database, that probability would be skewed, wouldn't it?"

"In theory, yes," Whitmore conceded. "But the overall impact would be minimal due to the high specificity of the STR loci we examined."

Satisfied, Gregg shifted gears. "DNA is a biological material that can be easily transferred from one person or object to another, isn't it?"

"Yes," Whitmore replied. "DNA can be transferred through direct contact or unintentional actions where they do not come into contact with the person."

"In your field, this is called indirect transfer, correct?"

"Correct."

"Indirect transfer means DNA can end up in a location without the person being physically present, doesn't it?"

"That's correct. This is referred to as secondary transfer."

"Could you explain how secondary transfer occurs?" Gregg asked.

"Certainly," Whitmore said. "For instance, if I touch a door handle, I leave my DNA on it. If someone else touches the same handle, they can carry my DNA on their hand and transfer it to another surface."

"So, it's possible for someone's DNA to appear at a location even if the person has never been there?"

"Yes, it's possible through secondary transfer."

Gregg nodded. "Let's discuss the handling of DNA evidence. Maintaining a strict chain of custody is essential, isn't it?"

"It's vital," Whitmore agreed. "The chain of custody ensures the evidence is handled and stored without contamination or tampering."

"What happens if the chain of custody is broken?" Gregg asked.

"It raises doubts about the evidence's integrity, including whether the sample has been contaminated or tampered with," Whitmore explained.

"And it's possible for someone to plant DNA at a crime scene, isn't it?"

"While highly unusual and unethical, it's theoretically possible," Whitmore admitted.

"DNA could also be transferred to a crime scene by someone other than the perpetrator, correct?"

"Yes, DNA could be transferred by someone else, such as a first responder, bystander, or an investigator if proper precautions aren't taken."

"In your professional experience, have you seen cases where someone's DNA was present at a scene or on an object found through innocent means?"

"Yes, it's not uncommon. For instance, a person's DNA can be found on an item they've never touched through secondary transfer or through casual contact with another person. We often find extraneous DNA at crime scenes, not knowing whose DNA it is or how it got there."

"And everyday actions at the crime scene—like an officer shaking another person's hand or an ambulance driver brushing against a bystander—can transfer DNA, correct?"

"Yes," Whitmore admitted.

"If someone happened by chance to be in a location where Mr. Jordan had been and then went to the crime scene, they could transfer his DNA there, couldn't they?"

"It's theoretically possible," Whitmore said. "But precautions are taken to minimize such risks."

"You say that, but you never were at this crime scene, were you?"

"No, I wasn't."

"Doctor, even if those in charge had taken precautions, you can't definitively say no extraneous DNA contaminated the scene, can you?"

"I can't," Whitmore conceded.

Gregg looked to deliver a final blow. "So, you can't confirm whether the DNA you analyzed, allegedly belonging to Mr. Jordan, was part of the crime scene or transferred there later, either intentionally or accidentally?"

Whitmore took a breath. "I can only say that if procedures were followed, the chances of such contamination are very low."

Gregg turned his back on the witness. "No further questions, Your Honor." He returned to the counsel table, exchanging a brief glance with Sam, who let out a quiet sigh of relief.

McBride stood. "The prosecution has no follow-up for this witness."

The judge looked at the clock. "Let's take our afternoon break. Jurors, please be back in your seats in fifteen minutes, and we'll continue with the next witness."

Chapter 48

NOT ALL WITNESSES ARE created equal. Each plays a distinct role in the courtroom puzzle—some are cornerstone pieces, anchoring the narrative, while others serve as smaller, supporting fragments that help hold the story together.

In trials, lawyers aim to start and end strong: an opening witness to paint the big picture and a closing witness to leave a lasting impression on the jury during deliberations. Witnesses called in the middle contribute smaller, less crucial details that tie the case together. They may not create fireworks, but they are vital for crafting a complete and compelling narrative.

The prosecution in this trial attempted a bold opening, showcasing their expert witnesses. Marcia McBride, determined to secure the conviction she desired, hoped their testimony had landed with the jury. Still, she knew her supporting witnesses were nearly as critical—providing key pieces of evidence to solidify her case.

"The prosecution calls Caspar T'Freigh," she announced.

A young man, perhaps in his early twenties, rose from the second row. Dressed in a slim-fitting suit, with dyed blond hair, he walked to the witness stand. He coughed three times while being sworn in, then sipped from a glass of water before sitting.

"Please tell the jury your name," McBride began.

"My name is Caspar T'Freigh." He spelled it for the court reporter. "It's pronounced 'T-Free.'"

"Where do you work?"

"I am a customer care provider at the Twin Pines Lodge."

"And what does that entail?"

"I work at the front desk, checking in guests and ensuring their stays are satisfactory."

McBride gestured toward the defense table. "On July 23 of last year, did you check in a man identifying himself as Samuel Jordan at the Twin Pines Lodge?"

"I did. It was early in the evening."

"Is that man seated in the courtroom today?"

T'Freigh scanned the courtroom and then settled his gaze on Sam, pointing at him. "That's the man."

"Let the record reflect," McBride said to the court reporter, "that the witness has identified the defendant, Samuel Jordan."

After a brief pause, she turned her attention back to the witness. "How do you remember that day?"

T'Freigh smirked. "I have a strong memory, but there were circumstances associated with his stay which helped me to remember it."

"What were those circumstances?"

"Well, the morning after Mr. Jordan checked in, I got a call from the cleaning staff. They said his room was a mess. I went upstairs to the room to check it out."

"What did you find?"

"There was a broken champagne bottle, and champagne had been sprayed all over the room. Broken glass also covered the floor. We had to bring in special cleaners for the carpets. It was quite a mess."

"Did you double-check the hotel records to confirm it was Mr. Jordan's room that was trashed?"

"Yes, I did. I verified he was assigned to that room. In fact, I was responsible for charging his credit card for the damage to the room."

"Did Mr. Jordan ever contact the hotel to dispute the charge or complain it was unauthorized?"

"Not that I'm aware of."

"Thank you, Mr. T'Freigh. No further questions."

Gregg rose slowly from his chair but stayed at counsel table. He only had a few questions.

"Mr. T'Freigh," Gregg began, "you never actually saw Mr. Jordan enter the room in question, correct?"

"That's correct, but I do remember giving him a key. He looked upset and even asked for a refund."

Gregg's expression tightened. "Please stick to answering my questions. You didn't see him enter the room, did you?"

"No, I didn't."

"And you didn't see him leave the hotel either, did you?"

"No, I didn't. My shift ended at midnight."

"So, you have no direct knowledge of what Mr. Jordan did before or after he supposedly checked into his room?"

"That's true. Other than giving him the key, I can't say anything about his actions."

"Thank you, sir, I have no further questions."

The witness left the stand, exiting the courtroom quietly. His testimony had added a brick to the wall McBride was building. She, however, had already turned her attention to preparing for her next witness.

Chapter 49

MARCIA MCBRIDE STOOD, HER back momentarily to the jury, her sharp gaze locking on Gregg as she offered him a sly wink. A shiver ran down his spine. "The prosecution calls Trevor Morrison," she announced.

Sam leaned closer to Gregg, his voice low and incredulous. "You've got to be kidding me. What the hell can he talk about?"

"They listed him as a potential witness," Gregg whispered back, his body tense. "We're about to find out." His eyes shifted to the back of the courtroom as the heavy doors creaked open.

After a momentary delay, a grown-up Trevor Morrison entered. He was dressed impeccably in a dark green suit, the rich fabric complementing his cream-colored shirt. The open collar added a touch of casual sophistication, avoiding anything too formal. His long auburn hair cascaded past his shoulders in loose waves. It had been years, but he seemingly was untouched by time, a mirror of the carefree lad he had once been.

Trevor walked confidently toward the witness stand, but stopped midway to embrace Gina, who stood and engulfed him in an immense hug. He touched her cheek before parting, allowing him to step forward and be sworn in. With practiced ease, he took his seat on the witness stand.

Marcia McBride wasted no time. "What is your name?"

"Trevor Morrison," he replied, offering the jurors a toothy grin.

"Where do you live?"

"Los Angeles, California."

"How do you know Gina Marcon?"

"We met at Camp Hershey about fifteen years ago," Trevor said, his voice lilting with a touch of nostalgia.

"Why are you here to testify?"

Trevor shrugged. "I'm not really sure. Gina called me a few weeks ago to tell me what happened to her husband. So, here I am."

McBride's expression didn't waver. "Tell us about your relationship with Gina."

Trevor's lips curved into a fond smile. "We spent one unforgettable summer together. She was wonderful and funny—one of those people who gives off an incredible energy. I suppose you could call us boyfriend and girlfriend. Whatever it was, it was a special summer."

"Did you know the defendant, Sam Jordan?"

Trevor nodded. "I did. We weren't close, but he seemed fine."

"Did he ever say anything to you about Gina or your relationship with her?"

Trevor hesitated, his brow furrowing. "Only once. One morning, down at the lake, we were just chatting. He was working there, and I had brought my kids to the water. He started asking about Gina and me, fishing for details. I kept things vague, but he didn't let up. Finally, he said—and I'm not even sure I was meant to hear— 'I would do anything to get with her.'"

McBride turned to the jury, her voice deliberate as she repeated, "'I would do anything to get with her.'" She let the words hang in the air before facing Trevor again. "Did you say anything to him about that comment?'

Trevor shook his head. "No. Honestly, I didn't think much of it at the time. I just figured she was out of his league and took it as a weird kind of compliment." He paused, before adding, "I never imagined it had any deeper meaning."

McBride let the silence linger, the weight of the testimony sinking in. Finally, she shifted her stance. "Mr. Morrison, have you seen Mrs. Marcon since that summer?"

"No. We lost touch and never reconnected." His gaze moved to Gina. "I'm so sorry for your loss." Gina's eyes glistened as she gave him a small, appreciative smile.

McBride nodded, signaling she was finished. "Your witness," she said, retaking her seat.

Gregg rose, his tone brisk. "Mr. Morrison, this conversation you say you had with Mr. Jordan at the lake happened fifteen years ago, correct?"

"Yes," Trevor confirmed.

"And you're not entirely sure you heard him correctly, are you?"

Trevor straightened in his seat. "I'm pretty sure I did."

"But aside from this alleged comment, you and Mr. Jordan never discussed Gina Szeka again, did you?"

"That's true."

"And you can't add one piece of relevant testimony about any-thing that has happened in the past fifteen years."

"I guess that's true."

"Nothing further," Gregg concluded, cool and detached.

Trevor stepped down from the stand, his movements graceful and unhurried. As he passed Gina, he placed a hand gently on her shoulder, then disappeared through the back doors of the courtroom, leaving a heavy silence in his wake.

Chapter 50

TRIALS OFTEN MOVED WITH the speed of a barge drifting down a river. If a bystander on the riverbank watched its progress, they would see movement, but the slow pace would eventually bore them by the time the barge disappeared around a bend.

Judge Denby's trials, however, proceeded at a much more brisk pace. While most judges allowed breaks to stretch longer than scheduled, Denby often had the jury back in the box ready for more testimony minutes before the break officially ended. Lawyers learned not to stray too far or face the prospect of returning to a silent courtroom with jurors already seated and the judge glaring down from the bench.

In his courtroom, days began early and testimony stretched late into the afternoon. Denby's intolerance for delays shaved days off trials. Though jurors often left exhausted, they appreciated being able to return to their lives sooner than expected.

Sam couldn't believe the prosecution's case was approaching its conclusion. The court had been informed two more witnesses would testify before the day ended: the victim's wife, Gina Marcon, and one final witness. Gregg objected when Denby extended the trial day to accommodate this, but the judge made it clear—he wanted the prosecution to finish before dismissing the jury for the day.

Gina sat in the gallery, her head held high with her hands clasped in her lap. She wore a near-black dress with lightweight sleeves, and her poised demeanor consumed Sam's attention despite his reluctance to look at her. He couldn't shake the feeling that she reveled in his discomfort.

Since Pablo's death, Gina had avoided all communication with Sam, and during the trial, they had shared the same courtroom without a single glance exchanged. This lack of interaction, while conspicuous, wasn't unexpected given the circumstances—he was accused of killing her husband. Even the jurors were aware of the tension.

"The prosecution calls Gina Marcon."

Gina stood and stared straight ahead, pausing for a moment before walking toward the witness stand. Her movements were deliberate, reminiscent of a bride walking down the aisle. Upon arriving, she tilted her head slightly upward before taking the oath.

Seated, she avoided looking at the jurors, fixing her attention instead on the prosecutor, who waited a moment before asking her first question. The courtroom was silent.

"What is your name?"

"Gina Marcon," she replied, her eyes cast downward.

The questioning continued with basic details: her residence, education, family background, and work history. As she answered, her responses gradually shifted to the jurors, allowing her to make tentative eye contact, as she transferred her gaze from one juror to the next.

"You are the wife of Pablo Marcon?"

"I was." Her voice cracked, and she broke eye contact, swiping her eyes.

"Tell us about him."

"I'm not sure where to start. He was amazing. We met about nine years ago. He was grounded, well-rounded, and really funny. Just amazing."

"Why do you say that?"

"He was a remarkable man. He always worried about me, always made sure I was okay. He started his own business making solar panels—it took a lot of time, but he built it into a huge success."

"Do you have any kids?"

Gina bit her lip and looked toward the ceiling. "We wanted to, desperately. We tried and tried, but nothing happened. I'm thirty-four. We were getting help, but now. . ., now it doesn't matter. We'll never—" She broke off, unable to finish. McBride handed her a tissue.

"Gina, what has your husband's murder done to your life?"

Gregg jumped to his feet. "Objection. Irrelevant and prejudicial."

The judge leveled a hard stare at Gregg. "Overruled. The jury will hear this testimony."

McBride nodded to Gina. "Mrs. Marcon, you may answer."

Gina's voice trembled. "My life is ruined. My dreams are destroyed. A good, decent man is dead—shot while he was in bed. I'll never understand how anyone could do this." She glared at Sam, who forced himself not to look away.

The jurors were riveted. Gina broke eye contact first, wiping a tear from her cheek.

McBride resumed. "Let's discuss your connection to the defendant, Sam Jordan. When did you first meet him?"

"Years ago, at a sleepaway camp. His attorney, Mr. Hubbard, was also there." She gestured toward Gregg, who remained impassive.

"Were you friends with Mr. Jordan?"

"I suppose. Everyone there was friendly. I talked to him, but we weren't particularly close."

"Were you and he boyfriend and girlfriend, or anything like that?"

She shook her head firmly. "Oh no, nothing like that. We were friendly, but that's all."

"Did he seem interested in more at the time?"

"If he did, I didn't know it."

McBride spoke in the direction of the jury. "So, you and Mr. Jordan didn't have contact for fifteen years?"

"Correct."

McBride pivoted. "You mentioned reconnecting with Mr. Jordan years later. How did that happen?"

"Through Facebook. His name popped up as someone I might know. I thought it was cool. I remembered him, so I sent him a message."

McBride handed Gina their text messages, previously marked as exhibits. Gina confirmed their authenticity and recounted how their conversations initially focused on catching up, before shifting in tone.

"Did you know he was separated from his wife?"

"I didn't. He never told me. He may have said something about having arguments, but I thought they were happy."

"Did he tell you that he was living in an apartment by himself?"

"No."

"What did he tell you about his work?"

"He sounded like he was a successful lawyer."

"Did he tell you he was working at his third law firm in a year, making less at each job?"

"He didn't."

"Mrs. Marcon, how would you characterize your texts with Mr. Jordan?"

"I don't know. They weren't much. He seemed like a nice guy. I didn't really know him when we were at camp. I thought we were friends, I guess."

"Did you and he ever talk by phone?"

"Yes. A few times."

"Why?"

"I don't know. It just seemed easier than texting. I was happy to hear from him. He sounded like he had a good life?"

"How many times did you talk?"

"Probably a few. I don't remember."

"Did anything happen as a result of the phone calls?"

"Well, we had found out that we lived less than two hours apart. He said he was going to be in my area for work and asked if I wanted to get something to eat?"

"What did you say?"

"I said, 'Yes.' I thought it would be fun?" She shook her head and rolled her eyes.

"Was it?"

"It started out normal. We talked and got some food, but then it got a little weird."

"How?"

"Towards the end of the evening, he started talking about coming back up and seeing me more. I think he said something about dating me. He talked a lot about how much he liked me back when we were at camp. I think he had too many to drink."

"So, what did you do?"

"By the end of the meal, I was uncomfortable. I told him I had a nice time, but I just got out of there."

"What did you do after you left?"

"I drove home. I live only a few minutes away from where we ate. Pablo was home. I had told him I was going to see an old friend. But when I walked in, I just started crying. I told him all about the dinner and how upset I was. He listened." She paused. "He was such a good listener."

"Did you and Mr. Jordan continue to have contact?"

"He tried to contact me."

"Describe for the jury the nature of the contact after your dinner."

"He texted a few times, but I didn't respond much. I steered the conversation to Pablo, so he understood my priorities. He called a few times, but I told him that I didn't think we should talk anymore. I told him I thought he had the wrong idea about me. After that, I stopped answering."

McBride took in a deep breath and said, "That's a lot. Tell me if this summary is true: You went to dinner with him one time. You left. You were a bit freaked out. You didn't want any more in-person contact."

"That's fair."

"Did you plan to see him after the first dinner?"

"No."

McBride walked back to her counsel table and stood next to it. "I would like to move onto the night of the murder. Do you need a break?"

Gina shook her head and bit her lip. "No, let's keep going."

McBride picked up a piece of paper. "I'm looking at the police report from the night your husband was shot. It says you called to report the shooting at 7:27 p.m. Is that correct?"

"That sounds about right."

"Will you take us back to earlier that evening before you made the 911 call."

Gina nodded. "I was at home. Pablo had a long day at work. I wanted to run to the mall to pick up a couple of things. He said he was going to lie down. He would do that sometimes. We were planning on having something to eat when I got back. It wouldn't take me long." She looked sheepishly at the jury. "Before I left, I popped upstairs to say goodbye. I guess he wasn't that tired, he made love to me."

She started to cry and grabbed another tissue. "That's the last time I ever saw him alive. I'm so glad we did it before I left."

The prosecutor paused, letting the jurors absorb her breakdown, and then asked,

"What time did you leave for the mall?"

Her brow furrowed. "It would have been a little after 6:15 that evening."

"What happened after you left the house?"

"I went to the mall and looked around for a while. Then I bought a sweater and a book."

McBride approached the witness stand. "I'm handing you what's been marked as Prosecution Exhibits 6 and 7. What are they?"

"They're the receipts for those two items."

"What time did you purchase them?"

She fumbled with the receipts. "On the first it says, 6:57 p.m., and on the other 7:12 p.m."

"Then what did you do?"

"My car was parked right outside the bookstore. It was an impulse buy. It only took a few minutes."

"Did you go straight home?"

"Yes. I was hungry and wanted to eat."

McBride walked over to her counsel table and riffled through some documents, but didn't pick any up. "What happened when you got home?"

Gina closed her eyes and sucked in a gulp of air before slowly letting it out. "I came in and threw the packages on the front table. I called out for Pablo because I assumed he fell asleep, and I knew he would want me to wake him up."

"What happened after that?"

"He didn't respond. I walked upstairs looking forward to spending a little time together." She paused appearing to gather her composure. "Our bedroom is right at the top of the steps. I opened the door, and I saw him. He was. . .."

The difficulty of further describing what she saw was apparent. She collected her thoughts. "He was sitting up in bed and his eyes were open, but something was wrong. Even from across the room I could see no life in his eyes. Then I saw blood above his head. I screamed and ran over to him. I knew I was too late, but I thought maybe I could get help. I called 911. You heard the call. I don't remember making it or anything that happened after." She reached for another tissue.

"Thanks Gina. I don't have any further questions."

The judge leaned forward to look at Gina. "Let's take a few minutes to stretch before cross-examination."

Chapter 51

GREGG STOOD IN FRONT of his counsel table, laser-focused on Gina, while the jury watched transfixed. Judge Denby appeared uninterested in their standoff, but the jurors remained motionless except for their eyes flicking back and forth between the two.

His mind wandered briefly to a memory of camp: Gina in a bathing suit, strolling along the beach, dark sunglasses masking her eyes, her long hair flowing in the wind. She had always been an enigma, keeping everyone at arm's length. Now, Gregg needed the jury to see her for who she truly was.

Her description of her relationship with Sam during her direct testimony could just as easily have described his own connection to her. Cool. Casual. Almost a friendship.

"He seemed like a nice guy, I guess, but we weren't close or anything like that," she'd said. That was Gina to a tee—nice on the surface but distant enough to keep people from truly getting to know her. It was as though she constantly held out a Heisman stiff arm, keeping others from getting too close.

Back then, she was an illusion. The unattainable "hot chick" everyone wanted to know, but no one truly did. Even after her testimony, Gregg realized he was no closer to understanding her. But if he was going to save Sam, he needed to find a way to shatter her façade.

"Mrs. Marcon, we are very sorry for your loss."

Gina murmured, "Thanks," but avoided Gregg's eyes, staring instead at the back wall of the courtroom.

"I want to ask you some questions about the night you found your husband shot in your bed."

She nodded, but still avoided looking at Gregg.

"You were home before you went to the mall, as you testified earlier. Is that correct?"

"Yes."

"And you were gone for less than fifty minutes?"

"Probably a little longer, but close."

"When you returned home, everything seemed normal?"

"Yes, I didn't notice anything unusual until I went upstairs."

Gregg held up the police report. "Just to confirm, you stated in this report that you locked all the doors before leaving, as was your usual practice, correct?"

"Yes, that's true."

"And when you returned, you entered through the locked garage door?"

"Yes."

"Nothing in the house was disturbed, and you had no indication anything was amiss until you discovered your husband upstairs?"

"Yes, that's correct."

Gregg paused, gesturing towards the prosecutor. "So, according to the prosecution's theory, Mr. Jordan entered your locked house, killed your husband, and left without leaving any trace—no broken windows, no forced doors, nothing disturbed."

"Apparently," Gina replied coolly.

"How, then, did Mr. Jordan gain access to your locked house?" Gregg pressed.

"I couldn't say," she answered, her tone flat.

Gregg leaned back. "The only plausible explanation is that your husband knew Mr. Jordan and willingly let him in. Isn't that correct?"

"I don't know. I can't say."

"That wouldn't make sense, though, would it? Your husband letting Mr. Jordan in, going back upstairs to bed, and then Mr. Jordan following him up to the bedroom to shoot him after he got back into bed?"

"I can't respond. I don't know," Gina said, her voice tightening.

Gregg raised his hands. "Understood. You can't explain how Mr. Jordan supposedly got into your house."

"I guess that's true," she conceded.

Shifting his position a few steps, Gregg said, "Let's move on to a different topic. You were the one who first contacted Mr. Jordan, weren't you?"

"I guess so," Gina muttered.

Gregg clicked a remote, and the screen displayed a text message: "Is this the Sam Jordan I knew long ago?"

"This was your message to him, correct? Mr. Jordan didn't initiate contact?"

"Yes, I sent it."

Gregg picked up a thick stack of documents. "These phone records, marked as Defense Exhibit B, show thirteen calls between you and Mr. Jordan. The calls ranged from four minutes to seventy-two minutes. Do you dispute that?"

Gina flipped through the pages briefly. "I don't remember the exact details, but if that's what the records say, I guess it's true." She waved the phone records and then placed them far to the side.

"Mrs. Marcon, you have neglected to tell the jury anything you and Mr. Jordan discussed in those phone calls."

She shook her head. "No, I haven't."

"Isn't it true, what you discussed in the phone calls was much different than what you said in your texts?"

"No!"

Gregg stepped closer. "What did you and Mr. Jordan talk about during those calls, particularly the seventy-two-minute one?"

"I don't remember specifics. We were catching up."

"Catching up?" Gregg arched an eyebrow. "That call was your ninth conversation. You were way past the 'catching up stage.' Weren't you discussing much more personal topics by then?"

"I don't think so," Gina scoffed.

"Weren't you suggesting to him that you and he should see each other more often?"

"No, I did not."

Gregg stood still, just shaking his head. "Two days later, you met him for dinner. Isn't that correct?"

"Yes."

A photograph of a cozy restaurant appeared on the screen. "This is where you had dinner, right?"

"I believe so."

"It's quite a romantic setting. Quaint, secluded, intimate even."

"It's just a restaurant," Gina retorted. "He picked it."

Gregg handed her a receipt. "Exhibit D shows that Mr. Jordan paid for dinner that night. You didn't offer to split the bill, did you?"

"I left before the bill arrived," Gina shot back.

"Let's move on." Gregg's tone turned sharper. "After that dinner, you and Mr. Jordan continued to talk, didn't you?"

"Not really. I told him I didn't want any more contact."

"But there were more calls, wasn't there?"

"A few. I told him to stop calling."

"In one of those calls, did you plan another dinner with him?"

Gina's face tightened. "Absolutely not. I told him he was misreading everything."

Gregg let the silence hang in the air before closing his folder. "Thank you, Mrs. Marcon. I have no further questions."

The frustration of a contentious cross-examination settled over Gregg like a heavy weight. Witnesses never conceded when it mattered most. Whether Gina's testimony was true or not, it starkly opposed the version of events Gregg needed the jury to hear. He had no idea which version they were believing.

Liz touched his arm to reassure him. "You gave them something to think about. An alternative perspective."

After hearing Gina's testimony, Gregg couldn't decide how much of it was real and what part she had made up on the spot. She had no discernible tell.

When Sam glanced back at Jenny sitting in the gallery, she wouldn't look at him. Instead, she turned her head and stared out the large window on the side of the courtroom.

Chapter 52

Harvey Spillman had been an officer since graduating from the academy twenty-two years earlier. Although his career lacked notable distinctions, he transitioned into investigative work. While not particularly adept, often leaning toward laziness rather than meticulousness, Spillman possessed one trait that endeared him to his department: he excelled on the witness stand.

Standing six-foot-two, with a full head of dark, curly hair and a perpetual two-day stubble, Spillman had the rugged good looks jurors might expect from a television detective. As a result of his confident demeanor, he received much more of the benefit of the doubt from juries than perhaps he deserved. His job was to close for the prosecution, to summarize the evidence for the jury, laying out the best version of the case, even if it occasionally meant stretching the bounds of reasonable interpretation to support their arguments.

McBride had already introduced Spillman to the jury, embellishing his career accomplishments to create an illusion of expertise. The jurors, swayed by his self-assured style, couldn't discern that he wasn't the superstar investigator he appeared to be. The presentation mattered more than the substance.

"What was your role in the investigation of this murder?" McBride asked.

Spillman waited until every juror's eye was on him before answering. "I am an internal evidence analyzer," he said, omitting the fact that this was, for the most part, a made-up job title. His primary responsibility was to organize evidence for jury presentation. Typically, he was the prosecution's final witness, providing a quasi-closing argument before the defense presented its case.

"My role is to review evidence and identify emerging patterns to assist detectives in solving the case," Spillman added.

"Did you do that in this case?" McBride asked.

"Of course. I reviewed all photographs, test results, and the communications between the victim's wife and the accused."

"Tell us about your review of the evidence."

Spillman nodded. "The first step was creating a timeline of events. Once we received the texts between Mr. Jordan and Mrs. Marcon, I analyzed the duration and content of their communications for insights into the events surrounding the murder."

"Did these communications provide any insights?"

"I believe they did."

"How?"

"The texts reveal significant evidence of Mr. Jordan's motive to murder Mr. Marcon."

Gregg jumped to his feet. "Objection, Your Honor. This line of testimony is speculative and prejudicial."

The judge peered at Gregg over his glasses. "It may be prejudicial, but it's relevant. You may cross-examine the witness to set the record straight." He gestured to McBride. "Please continue counselor."

McBride offered a smile at Gregg, who glared in return. "How does the timeline inform us?"

"We made a chart showing when the texts were made. I also included the phone calls. Obviously with the texts we have the exact words used. With the phone calls we only have when they were made and their duration."

"Referring to your chart, please walk the jury through the timeline."

Spillman activated a laser pointer, directing the beam toward a chart displayed on a screen. "The communication began on July 1st, initiated by a text from Mrs. Marcon to Mr. Jordan. His immediate response indicated enthusiasm for continuing their exchanges."

The ensuing texts on the screen scrolled by as the jurors stared enraptured by the amount of texting. Spillman didn't call out much of the text until he came to some about two weeks after the initial texts.

Spillman highlighted a message from July 7th. "This one stood out. It's from Mr. Jordan: 'Would love to get dinner with you. I'm alone most of the time I'm not at work. Would you want to meet?'"

He paused before continuing. "Mrs. Marcon didn't reply to this text immediately. Two days later, Mr. Jordan texted again: 'Hey, wondering if you're up to getting dinner some night. I'm not that far from you and have a work assignment near your area. Let me know. I think it would be lots of fun.'"

"Did Mrs. Marcon respond?" McBride asked.

"She did, but a day later. She wrote, 'That would be nice. Maybe my husband should come along?' Mr. Jordan discouraged the idea, replying, 'Nah, he wouldn't find it as much fun as we would. He wouldn't appreciate the camp stories. This would be so much more fun alone.'"

"How did Gina respond to that text?"

"She insisted on transparency, replying, 'Okay, but next time he should come. He always likes meeting new people.' She wasn't planning to hide the meeting from her husband."

"Did they meet at the restaurant?"

"Yes. While there are no texts explicitly arranging the meeting, phone records show calls between them in the days prior. Additionally, we have a receipt from Mr. Jordan's credit card confirming payment for their dinner."

"What other evidence confirms Mr. Jordan's presence?"

Spillman's smile returned. "His EZ Pass records show he left his home and exited the toll road near the restaurant, which is also close to Mrs. Marcon's house."

"Did they meet for a second dinner?"

"No evidence suggests they did. Communication between them diminished significantly after the first dinner. Mrs. Marcon's texts indicate she was uninterested in further interaction."

"Where was Mrs. Marcon on the night of the murder?"

"Her credit card and mall receipts place her at the mall during the time of the murder."

"And Mr. Jordan? Where was he on the night of the murder?"

Spillman's smug expression returned. "His credit card, cell phone, and toll records place him within two miles of the Marcons' home during the time of the murder."

"Can you elaborate?"

"The time of death has been put at some time after 6:30 p.m. The toll records show he entered the area near the Marcon residence at 5:33 p.m., over an hour before the estimated time of death, and left at 8:07 p.m., after the murder." Spillman grabbed the cup of water next to him and took a swig before continuing. "The toll records establish Mr. Jordan's presence in the area of the murder at the time of the murder."

"What did his credit card information establish?"

"Again, in review of his transactions, receipts indicate he was at the Pine Ridge hotel before the time of the murder. We obtained the restaurant invoice correlated with the credit card which established he purchased a drink at the restaurant an hour before the murder.

"In addition, the hotel's information I reviewed indicates that Mr. Jordan reserved and paid for a hotel room that evening. As you heard from the previous testimony, Mr. Jordan obtained a key to the room. There were later reports of a broken champagne bottle in the room that night.

"Given that the hotel is a three-minute drive from where the Marcons live, there was plenty of time to travel to the house before the time of the murder. Also, in light of the fact that there was broken glass in the hotel room, it's not difficult to imagine how Mr. Jordan's blood was left at the crime scene when Mr. Jordan arrived."

Spillman walked up to the line of objectionable testimony without quite going over it. He never said that Sam committed the murder, but his testimony established his presence in the area with sufficient time to commit the crime.

McBride continued, "What does his cell phone data reveal?"

"It's similar to the other information in that it showed him in the area of the crime." He pointed at Sam. "The nearest cell tower is less than a mile from the restaurant and the Marcon residence. Records from the cell provider indicate this tower transmitted his texts and calls and, therefore, was the closest tower."

"Thank you, Officer Spillman. One more area of inquiry." She paused and faced the jury while asking, "Did your review of the documents provide any additional information about Mr. Jordan's motive?"

Spillman nodded and tapped his fingers together. "Yes. His texts suggest that despite Mrs. Marcon never providing him any reason to believe her marriage was unhappy, he believed eliminating Mr. Marcon would allow him to pursue an intimate relationship with her."

Gregg shot out of his chair. "Objection. Move to strike. He's trying to read my client's mind. Speculation."

McBride countered, "He's only interpreting the defendant's texts. There's nothing improper here."

The judge adjusted his glasses. "You're treading close to the line, counselor. Don't cross it. Objection overruled."

McBride turned her attention back to the witness. "Why do you say that he believed he could pursue an intimate relationship with Mrs. Marcon?"

Spillman couldn't help but smirk. "Mr. Jordan's texts are filled with suggestions about spending time alone and questions about the state of Mrs. Marcon's marriage. While Mrs. Marcon gave no indication her marriage was unhappy, Mr. Jordan's actions and words suggest he wanted more."

"Thank you, Officer Spillman. No further questions."

Denby turned to Gregg. "Cross-examination?"

"Thank-you, Your Honor." Gregg rose, leaning against his table. "Officer Spillman, you weren't present at the crime scene, were you?"

"No, I wasn't. That's not my job."

"And you're not an expert in DNA?"

"No, but I can review DNA reports." Spillman said, sneering at Gregg.

"Prepared by actual experts." Gregg sneered back.

"Correct."

"You didn't interview any witnesses or collect any evidence, did you?"

"No. My role is to review and analyze the collected evidence."

"You didn't even prepare the timeline shown to the jury, did you?"

"True. I delegated that task but ensured its accuracy."

"In short, Officer Spillman," Gregg spit out his name, "you conducted no investigation and presented no new information today."

"Well, like I said before," Spillman offered his toothiest smile to the jury, "my job is to interpret information collected in the course of an investigation, in this case, the murder of Pablo Marcon. I hope I was able to condense the information already collected and explain it in a logical and informative manner to the jury."

Frustrated at his inability to wipe the sneer off Spillman's face, Gregg sat down, muttering, "No further questions."

McBride rose and said in the jury's direction, "The prosecution rests."

The judge turned to the jury. "We've had a productive day. We'll reconvene tomorrow morning for the defense's case."

The jurors nodded, and, without a sound, filed out.

Chapter 53

S AM GLARED, HIS FACE reddened, his mouth twisted as he barked, "I want to testify."

Gregg turned his back, giving himself a moment to gather his thoughts.

The courtroom had emptied after the prosecution's last witness; the jurors had departed, leaving the space quiet. The court staff allowed Gregg to speak privately with his client, while the officer assigned to escort prisoners back to jail waited in the hallway. Jenny and Sam's mom wanted to stay, but they were told they wouldn't be able to speak with Sam after the meeting. Gregg shooed them out, reassuring them that they would talk more in the morning.

And then it got ugly.

Gregg seated Sam at their counsel table and methodically reviewed the witnesses who had testified so far, explaining that they lacked evidence to counter the prosecution's claims. He went over the DNA evidence, pointing out the weaknesses he had exposed in their testimony, but also conceding it was nearly impossible to dispute that Sam's DNA had been found at the scene. The mere mention of this caused Sam to kick over the chair beside him.

"If they think I was at the house, I'm cooked! I'm done if I can't convince them I wasn't."

They argued for several minutes before Sam declared that he wanted to take the stand.

"You can't," Gregg countered.

"It's the only way to convince them I had nothing to do with this!"

Gregg shook his head. "It's the surest way to guarantee they'll convict you in under an hour."

"You don't know what they'll do."

"I do," Gregg snapped, his voice trembling. "We were taught in law school to never let a criminal defendant testify. I've followed that rule my entire career, and it's never failed me. Testifying opens doors for an experienced prosecutor. She'll dance through each one."

"And how many of your clients were found not guilty?" Sam sneered.

"A few. But I can guarantee you that all of them would still be behind bars if they had testified."

"I'm different. I didn't kill anyone."

"You don't have to remind me," Gregg replied, gazing at the ceiling as if seeking divine intervention. "If you testify, the prosecutor will pounce. She'll reintroduce all the DNA evidence, piece by piece. And what will you say? 'It's rigged,' or 'It's wrong?' You'll sound desperate. She'll dredge up your texts with Gina and let the jury linger on how much you wanted to be with her. Then she'll fabricate conversations from your phone records. She'll ask,

'Didn't you tell Mrs. Marcon you wanted her husband out of the way?' or 'Didn't you say you'd do anything to be with her?'"

"It's all lies!"

Gregg shook his head. "Is it? It doesn't matter. She can ask anything, planting doubts and painting a narrative the jurors won't forget. Your denials won't carry the same weight as her accusations."

"I wasn't there."

"I know. But putting you on the stand only gives her more ammunition. You'll be vulnerable, and I won't be able to protect you."

Sam stared at the floor, muttering, "The truth has to matter."

Gregg placed a reassuring hand on his shoulder. "It does, buddy. But sometimes the truth the jury decides on isn't the real truth. My job is to do what's best for you."

"Feels like I lose either way."

The officer peeked into the courtroom. "I have to take him back now."

Gregg flashed him a thumbs-up. "You have to tell me what you want to do. It's your decision. I can't make it for you, I can only offer you advice."

"I'm glad you're looking out for me. The frustration of listening to all this crap is killing me. It's making me want to scream." He slumped far down into his chair and grabbed his face with his hands, and wailed, "You win. I won't testify." He looked up, his eyes sunken and sallow, his bottom lip quivering, shoulders hunched, his whole-body sagging. "You better be right, buddy."

Chapter 54

REMINISCENT OF HIS FIRST day of law school, Gregg's stomach churned relentlessly. He and Sam walked out of the judge's chambers, trailed by Marcia McBride and her team. Gregg noted absently that her minions were the same height and always walked side by side—like out of a Dr. Suess book. He shook his head—such details were irrelevant now. What mattered was that he had put on the record that his client had waived his right to testify and that the defense would not be presenting any evidence.

This strategy wasn't unusual. Defense attorneys often argued that the prosecution's evidence was either insufficient or tainted, failing to meet the burden of proof. Gregg had employed this strategy numerous times; occasionally, it succeeded, and his clients walked free. But the approach carried risks. If he had direct exculpatory evidence, he would present it. He didn't. His case rested on convincing the jury that Marcia McBride, with all her confidence and air of superiority, had failed to prove Sam was the killer.

Back in the courtroom, Gregg and Sam returned to their seats as the jurors were ushered in. Judge Denby addressed them with measured authority.

"When we left yesterday, the prosecution had finished presenting its evidence and rested its case. It is now the defendant's opportunity to present evidence. I have been informed by Mr. Hubbard that the defendant will not present any evidence. Is this accurate, counselor?"

Gregg stood. "It is, Your Honor."

Denby turned to the jurors. "Jury members, the defendant in this case has chosen not to testify. Under the laws of the United States and the Commonwealth of Pennsylvania, a defendant has an absolute right not to testify. It is their decision whether to take the stand in their own defense or present evidence.

"You must not draw any inference or reach any conclusion about the defendant's guilt or innocence based on this choice. The decision is not evidence of guilt and should not influence your deliberations. Remember, the defendant is presumed innocent unless proven guilty beyond a reasonable doubt. The burden of proof rests solely with the Commonwealth and never shifts to the defendant. The fact the defendant chooses not to testify does not relieve the Commonwealth of its burden of proving each element of the charges against the defendant beyond a reasonable doubt.

"Your verdict must be based on the evidence presented and my instructions on the law. The decision not to testify must not factor in your judgment or verdict. I will reiterate this in my final charge."

The jurors remained impassive.

Denby continued, "With the close of evidence, it is now time for the attorneys to deliver their closing arguments. Remember, their arguments are not evidence. You are the judges of the evidence, and your recollection of it—not the attorneys'—should guide your deliberations."

He looked at Gregg. "Under the law, counsel for the defendant gives the first closing argument. The prosecution, because it has the burden of proof, will close last. Mr. Hubbard, are you prepared to proceed?"

Gregg rose. "I am. Thank you, Your Honor."

Striding to the jury box, Gregg carried nothing with him—no notes, no exhibits. His goal was to appear sincere and unencumbered. Resting a hand on the railing, he began, his voice steady but impassioned.

"You hold the fate of a good man in your hands—a working man with a son and a wife." He gestured to Jenny and Sam's mother, who raised their eyes to meet the jurors'. "A man who may have made some poor choices in his life, but a man who never committed the crime the prosecutor accuses him of."

He pointed at McBride, catching a faint smirk at the corner of her lips. "The Commonwealth's case is built entirely on circumstantial evidence. Once you examine it closely, it collapses like a house of cards."

Gregg met each juror's gaze, drawing strength from their focus. "One man has already lost his life—a tragedy. Mr. Marcon was unfairly taken from this world, and we all sympathize deeply with Mrs. Marcon." He turned toward Gina, who stared at the floor, avoiding his eyes.

"We all crave justice for this heinous crime. We want to lash out and find someone to punish. But justice must be precise. You cannot punish the wrong person." A couple of jurors nodded, so he spoke to them. "You must be absolutely certain—not just think you're right, but you must know it beyond any reasonable doubt."

He paused for emphasis. "'Beyond a reasonable doubt'—a high standard. If any of you has any doubt about Mr. Jordan's guilt, you must acquit him."

Gregg stepped closer. "The prosecution's case is riddled with reasonable doubt, from its failure to consider any other suspects, to the evidence it presented, all raising more questions than answers.

"Let's start with what they don't have. No murder weapon. No witness placing Mr. Jordan at the scene. No evidence he was ever near the Marcon home. Even with all the witnesses they paraded in here, none said that Mr. Jordan was ever in the house.

"And the story they've constructed doesn't add up. There was no forced entry. Mrs. Marcon testified she locked all the doors when she left, and they were locked when she returned. Nothing was stolen. Nothing was disturbed. How did Mr. Jordan enter the house? Mr. Marcon didn't know him, had never met him, and wouldn't have let him in." He stared at the jurors. "That is reasonable doubt."

"Mr. Marcon was in bed. There is no evidence he ever got out of bed. They're suggesting Mr. Marcon answered the door, invited Mr. Jordan up to his bedroom and then got back into bed before Mr. Jordan entered the bedroom and shot him. It doesn't make any sense.

"They have no gun." He pointed at McBride. "The prosecution has no evidence Mr. Jordan ever owned a gun, and no record of him ever purchasing one. No evidence of him borrowing one. Nothing. Without the murder weapon, there's no link between my client and the crime. More reasonable doubt."

Gregg paced in front of the jury box signaling a shift in his argument. "Let's talk about the DNA evidence. We've all seen TV shows that portray DNA as infallible. But the truth is far more complicated. Testing is a meticulous, multi-step process prone to human error. Any misstep—from the collection at the scene, to the handling of the evidence, to the testing in the lab—can result in contamination or errors. The prosecution's own expert admitted they didn't follow their own procedures. Can we trust their results? Absolutely not."

"Think about how easy it would be for a single misplaced cell, a sneeze, or perhaps a minor procedural slip to taint the results. Can we be sure, beyond a reasonable doubt, the evidence chain here was followed without any error? Absolutely not.

"Further, let's talk about lab procedures. Labs vary in their quality and reliability, and errors happen all the time. Contamination happens. They put significant pressure on technicians to produce results which support the prosecution's narrative. This pressure leads to biases in reading the results or interpreting mixed samples in ways which unfairly point to a suspect." Gregg pointed at the jurors. "You can't convict my client based on this flawed testing."

He paused to take a sip of water. "Ask yourself: Did the prosecution give us a clear chain of custody? DNA is incredibly fragile. It can degrade, be transferred from one place to another, or even accidentally brought to a crime scene by someone else. You heard all the testimony about secondary transfer, and how someone else's DNA can be brought into a crime scene without anyone knowing it happened.

"They say Sam was in the restaurant near to the crime scene. Did the lead investigator ever check to determine how many of the people who ended up at the crime scene may have been in the restaurant before traveling to the crime scene? They didn't. We just don't know if someone was in the restaurant and without knowing it, brought Sam's DNA to the Marcon house. How can we be certain this DNA wasn't introduced by secondary transfer?"

The jurors stared at Gregg. "You can't convict someone based on DNA evidence," he continued, "when this evidence might have been brought to the scene by someone else. Even if Sam's DNA evidence was at the scene, this doesn't mean Sam was at the house and certainly doesn't mean he committed murder.

"In this case, there is too much room for doubt. With such a high-stakes decision, we cannot afford the luxury of blindly relying on DNA results which are vulnerable to human error. The question here is not whether DNA can match, but whether we can trust it matched my client's DNA beyond a reasonable doubt. I urge you to recognize the doubt in this evidence."

Sam turned his back on the jurors and paced back to his counsel table. He stopped and then faced them again. He placed a hand on Sam's shoulder. "This is an innocent man. Doubt is screaming at you. Justice demands the truth. Find him 'not guilty.'"

Gregg returned to his seat. Denby nodded. "The prosecution will deliver its closing argument after the break."

Chapter 55

MARCIA MCBRIDE DELAYED BEFORE rising, wanting every eye to be on her before proceeding. The courtroom remained still, a collective hush hanging over it. She stood, her toned legs displayed beneath her grey, tailored suit.

She picked up a stack of documents and walked to the podium before the jurors, who edged forward in their seats. "Ladies and gentlemen," she began, "we have presented you with a case built on science, logic, and undeniable truth. This case proves that Sam Jordan, in cold blood, murdered Pablo Marcon on the night of July 23, while Mr. Marcon lay in bed.

"We've shown you a crime scene littered with Mr. Jordan's DNA, conclusively establishing his presence there. This shouldn't come as a surprise, given that we've also proven Mr. Jordan was at the Oakley Restaurant and the Pine Ridge Hotel earlier that evening, where he broke a champagne bottle less than an hour before the murder."

She paused, letting her words settle in the room.

"Think about this. Mr. Jordan had no reason to be two hours away from his home, just minutes from Gina Marcon's residence. No reason, except for what we've proven—to commit murder.

"So, we've established that Mr. Jordan was in the same town as Mr. Marcon, and his DNA was found in the blood spatter and beneath Mr. Marcon's fingernails. Yet, the defense has failed to offer any explanation for his presence there, other than the one we've proven: he was there to kill Mr. Marcon."

She took a step closer to the jury box. "Certain facts remain undisputed. Mr. Marcon was shot in the head and chest while lying in bed." On the screen, grisly photographs of Pablo Marcon's bloodied body appeared. "He can't speak to you. He has no voice in this courtroom. But Mr. Jordan's DNA speaks for him."

She turned, pointing at Sam Jordan. "The defense wants you to disregard science. They want you to believe there's some chance the crime scene was contaminated, despite no evidence to support this claim. Investigators testified to the care they took in preserving and documenting evidence at the scene. They compiled everything in a meticulous and professional manner, yet the defense seeks to impugn their integrity in a vain attempt to create baseless doubt about the critical conclusions this evidence leads us to."

Her voice grew resolute. "Ladies and gentlemen, science does not lie. DNA doesn't randomly appear at crime scenes. It doesn't magically leap from innocent bystanders to victims. The DNA found in Pablo Marcon's blood and at the very spot where he took his last breath is the silent witness speaking louder than any word he might utter. No, we didn't recover the gun that shot

Mr. Marcon—but we don't need it. The presence of Sam Jordan's DNA conclusively establishes who wielded the murder weapon."

She gestured toward the jury. "You heard from our expert DNA witness, Alan Whitmore—a man with impeccable qualifications, whose testimony went unchallenged by the defense. He testified that there's less than a one-in-a-billion chance the DNA found at the scene didn't belong to Sam Jordan. It was his DNA, and the only way it got there was because he was inside the house.

"The evidence is irrefutable. Sam Jordan's credit card records establish he was near the Marcon residence. His DNA proves he was inside it."

Her gaze swept over the jury. "Now, let's talk about motive. While we don't need to prove motive to establish guilt, it's the final puzzle piece that not only confirms Mr. Jordan's actions but explains why he committed this heinous crime."

The text messages between Sam and Gina appeared on the screen. "Sam Jordan was infatuated with Gina Marcon. She reached out to him, wanting to rekindle a friendship, but he saw it as an opportunity to make her his lover—despite her repeatedly affirming the strength of her marriage and giving him no reason to believe she wanted anything more than friendship.

"Sam Jordan's life was crumbling. His wife had kicked him out. His career was failing. His relationship with his child in ruins. Desperate for a lifeline, he latched onto Gina as his best hope."

"In his twisted, depraved mind," she said, her voice tinged with disdain, "he believed that if Pablo Marcon were out of the picture, Gina would be his. He convinced himself that killing Pablo would be his salvation. Blinded by this delusion, he was willing to kill for it."

Her voice rose again, gaining power. "The DNA doesn't lie." She pointed at Sam while locking eyes with the jury. "Sam Jordan murdered Pablo Marcon. And you are the only ones who can ensure Pablo Marcon's voice is heard, and that justice is served."

She took a final breath. "I ask you, don't let the silence of a missing weapon obscure the undeniable voice of the evidence. Return a verdict of guilty and grant Pablo Marcon the justice he deserves. Thank you."

The courtroom was silent as she returned to her seat. Behind her, Gina Marcon sobbed uncontrollably, her body heaving as she struggled to compose herself.

Chapter 56

A FTER A SHORT BREAK, Judge Denby turned to the jurors. "Members of the jury, now that you have received all the evidence and heard counsel's closing arguments, it is my duty to instruct you on the law governing this case. I will also guide you on how to handle your deliberations and reach a verdict. You are the judges of the facts; I am the judge of the law, and you must accept the law as I give it to you."

Gregg listened intently, double-checking to ensure Denby covered every instruction as agreed upon the evening before. Crafting appropriate instructions had been a tedious process. Both sides had submitted proposed language, which the judge reviewed before meeting with counsel to finalize his charge. Like most judges, Denby aimed for instructions that fairly encompassed the law while minimizing potential avenues for appeal.

"First," Denby continued, "remember, the defendant is presumed innocent." Gregg checked off "presumed innocent" from his list. "This presumption remains with the defendant unless and until you are convinced the Commonwealth has proven the defendant guilty beyond a reasonable doubt. The burden of proving each element of the charges rests entirely with the Commonwealth. The defendant is not required to prove innocence or present any evidence."

Gregg's ears perked up as Denby moved to the concept of reasonable doubt—the crux of their defense.

"Now, let me explain what we mean by 'beyond a reasonable doubt.' This does not mean proof beyond all doubt or to a mathematical certainty. It means you must be firmly convinced of the defendant's guilt based on the evidence presented. If, after considering all the evidence, you have a reasonable doubt as to the defendant's guilt, you must return a verdict of 'not guilty.' Conversely, if you are firmly convinced of the defendant's guilt, you should find the defendant 'guilty.'"

Mentally, Gregg reviewed the arguments he had presented to raise reasonable doubt and offered a prayer they were sufficient. Denby then addressed the specific charges. The prosecution had charged Sam with three counts of murder: first-degree, second-degree, and manslaughter.

The judge began with the elements of first-degree murder. "For first-degree murder, you must find that the killing was intentional, willful, deliberate, and premeditated. This means the defendant made a conscious decision to kill and had time to think before acting, even if the time was brief."

Although Denby explained the elements of the lesser charges afterward, Gregg was convinced that if the jury convicted Sam, it would be for first-degree murder. If they believed Sam had driven to Gina's house intending to kill Pablo, they would also conclude his actions were intentional, willful, deliberate, and premeditated. No middle ground existed; either Sam would walk out a free man or face decades in prison.

The final instructions were standard in any criminal trial. "You are also the sole judges of the facts and the credibility of each witness. When assessing a witness's credibility, you may consider their demeanor, how their testimony aligns with other evidence, and whether they have any bias or interest in the case's outcome. You may accept all, part, or none of any witness's testimony as you see fit."

Denby emphasized that the jurors should consider only the evidence presented during the trial and not be influenced by factors outside the courtroom. He instructed them to deliberate with an open mind and approach their task thoughtfully.

Lastly, he reminded them their verdict had to be unanimous. Looking at the jurors, who were giving him their full attention, he explained the procedure for submitting questions to the court and how to return with their verdict once one was reached.

It's always a solemn moment when a jury leaves the courtroom to begin deliberating on the fate of another human. Gregg watched them file out, their expressions giving no hint of what they were thinking—just as in most cases he had tried.

Chapter 57

G REGG ARRIVED AT THE courthouse early, eager to decompress before the day's events. The jury had begun deliberating the afternoon before, but no one expected them to reach a decision before Denby dismissed them, instructing them to return in the morning.

The previous day, Jenny and Sam's mom had stayed for the first hour of deliberation, but Gregg suggested they leave, explaining that no decision would be made until the following day.

As a criminal defendant in custody, Sam had to wait in a holding cell until the jury reached a verdict. The uncertainty of waiting for any verdict is a form of psychological torture, with perhaps the best psychological comparison being waiting for a loved one to get out of a major surgery.

In Gregg's past trials, he had spent countless hours agonizing over the jury's decision, each minute dragging on as he mentally replayed every possible mistake he had made during the trial. It was brutal, but it paled in comparison to the hell Sam was enduring, wondering if he would be set free or face years behind bars, all while confined to a dank holding cell, no bigger than a broom closet.

With his computer open, Gregg tried to send some emails but struggled to focus. Exhaustion had taken its toll on his sleep-deprived body. At least while the jury deliberated, he didn't need to prepare for any cross-examinations, so he could be in bed before midnight.

Liz arrived, looking far more put together than Gregg felt. Being second chair had its perks. Sure, she had spent countless hours on witness outlines and last-minute research, but it was the person in the first chair who bore the greatest burden. He was the one who would receive credit for the victory, but also suffer most from the sting of a defeat.

They hadn't seen the jurors arrive, but just a few minutes before they were due to start, Jenny and Sam's mom appeared. A woman in her early sixties, she seemed to have aged ten years since the trial began. Gregg had known her since high school but seeing her under the stress of her son's trial made her almost unrecognizable.

"How long do you think it'll take?" Jenny asked, sounding flat and devoid of emotion.

Gregg shook his head. "I don't know. Sometimes they reach a decision quickly, sometimes it takes longer. The amount of time they take doesn't tell us anything about which way they're leaning. It's all a guess."

Jenny placed a hand on Sam's mom's arm. "Rebecca had a question."

Rebecca turned to Gregg, her weary eyes glistening with unshed tears. "How long would his sentence be?"

Gregg sighed. "I don't think now is the time to talk about that. Let's just send positive thoughts to the jury, so we never have to answer that question."

Rebecca stood and moved toward Gregg, sitting across from him. "Gregg, I'm not sure if I've told you how much I appreciate everything you've done for Sam. We'd be lost without you." She reached into her bag, pulled out a tissue, and twisted it in her hand. "You remember when Sam's dad died? You were in college. It was so sudden. For years, I was lost, like I was sleepwalking. Having Sam around helped me keep going. I moved to Arizona a few years ago, but if it hadn't been for Sam, I don't think I would have made it."

She dabbed at her eyes with the tissue. "If I lose Sam, who's going to help me get through this?" She stared straight ahead, then let out a gut-wrenching sob. Jenny wrapped her arm around Rebecca's shoulders, easing her head onto her own.

Gregg watched, unable to offer any words of comfort.

They waited for hours, with only an occasional word exchanged among them. None of them could stand the thought of eating, each puttering away time, trying to find any means of distraction.

By mid-afternoon they all believed they were losing their minds, not knowing how long until Sam learned his fate. A knock at the door interrupted their stupor. Judge Denby's tipstaff poked her head inside. "We have a verdict."

Rebecca let out a nearly inaudible gasp while Jenny stood and placed a hand on her shoulder.

"The jury will be brought back in ten minutes." The tipstaff ducked out.

Gregg bit his lower lip and led the group out of the conference room. No one said a word.

Chapter 58

G REGG HAD TRIED A few smaller civil cases since entering private practice. Most criminal attorneys dip their toes into civil law, attempting to win personal injury cases for friends or lease disputes for former clients. The stress of waiting for a jury to return in a civil case, where the only issue is the payment of money, can be significant. However, that anxiety pales in comparison to waiting for a criminal verdict, with the possibility that the client could serve time in jail. For the families of criminal defendants, the consequences of a felony conviction can tear them apart.

And despite how unnerving the wait can be while a jury deliberates, the time between hearing that a decision has been reached, and the actual reading of the verdict is the ultimate torture.

Rebecca Jordan had watched her sister die of leukemia at a young age, lived on the brink of poverty growing up, and lost her husband years before she was ready to say goodbye. These events nearly destroyed her, but the minutes spent waiting for the jury's decision were infinitely more fraught. She sat two rows behind Sam, who had been brought into the courtroom a few minutes earlier with a brief nod at his mother. Her face was pale, her eyes rimmed red from days of solitary crying. She wanted to make eye contact with her son one more time, but all she saw was the back of his head.

Without a word, the jurors filed in through the door at the front of the courtroom. They kept their eyes straight ahead, offering no hint of their decision. The first juror carried a sheet of paper—the verdict slip—in her hand. In stark black and white, it held Sam's already determined fate.

Rebecca strained forward, longing to touch her son, but he was too far away. She leaned further, but it was futile.

Judge Denby, noting the jury was in position, turned toward them and asked, "Have you reached a decision?"

Juror No. 1, her brown hair streaked with gray and her gaze steady, stood and announced, "We have."

"What sayeth the jury?"

Juror No. 1 glanced at the verdict slip as if she hadn't already memorized its contents. Her hands trembled. "We find the defendant, Samuel Jordan, guilty of first-degree murder."

Bile rose in Rebecca's throat, and she thought she would gag. Instead, an uncontrolled yelp escaped her mouth. She threw her hand up to muffle the sound, but it only devolved into a low moan that spread through the courtroom.

Sam turned to his mother, his eyes sagging, mouth agape. He couldn't muster a word. Gregg placed an arm over his shoulder but, like his friend, found no words to offer. He collected himself and asked the judge to poll the jurors.

Denby asked each juror if this was their verdict, and after each juror agreed, Sam's fate was sealed.

Sitting next to Rebecca, Jenny stared straight ahead, her face devoid of expression, her hands clenched together in her lap.

Denby turned his attention from the jury and to Sam. "Mr. Jordan, the jury has found you guilty of first-degree murder. You will be removed from the courtroom, remanded back into custody, and returned to your cell. Sentencing will occur in two weeks."

As Sam stood, he turned one last time to his mother, his eyes now welling. She mouthed, "I love you," her voice barely audible over her breaking sobs. He nodded, unable to speak, and was led out of the courtroom, leaving her alone with Jenny to contemplate his fate and their uncertain futures.

Chapter 59

B EFORE HIS TRIAL, SAM at least had the hope his torture would end. Being alone in his cell, day after day, ate away at his mental stability. Before, with the hope of a jury acquittal, he had some expectation that it would eventually end and his life would return to a semblance of normal. Not now. Not since the jury had found him guilty of murder. Murder. Killing another person. Taking the life of Gina's husband. None of it was true, but each juror believed it. They thought he had held a gun to Pablo's head and pulled the trigger.

Every night, lying on his lumpy mattress, his mind conjured images of brains splattering on the wall, and blood pooling on the sheets. The vivid, horrific images forced their way into his thoughts. And now, knowing that the jury believed he had caused that scene, made him seethe with anger. They thought he was capable of cold-blooded murder. They had no idea, and they didn't care.

He relived the trial—witness by witness—picking apart everything Gregg had said, obsessing over each argument the slimy prosecutor had made. She cared nothing for the truth; her willingness to misrepresent the evidence violated her ethical obligations to the court—and Sam had caught her winking at Gregg more than once.

Was his lawyer sleeping with the prosecutor? Was that her plan all along? Get in deep with Gregg and find out how he would try the case. What a slut. She just wanted a conviction and didn't care about the truth. Now, because of her ambition, he was going to rot away in jail.

Sam's grievance grew with each passing day. With little to do other than stew in his cell, there was no chance his sense of indignation would subside. In the week since the verdict, he hadn't spoken to any family or friends. Gregg had visited, but Sam refused to see him. Instead, he told the guard to give him the following message: "You're a traitor. You failed me. Because of you, I'm going to rot away in jail."

Gregg's response came: "I'll be back in a week. Hopefully, we can talk then."

Sam ripped up the note and flushed it down the toilet.

As he lay on his bed, wallowing in his despair, Mike, the guard he now considered his only real friend, tapped on the door. Sam rolled over toward him. "What's up?"

Mike leaned against the bars. He was a towering presence, but he made an effort not to use his physicality to threaten the inmates. "You got a visitor."

Sam exhaled loudly. "Tell him I don't want him here."

"It's not your lawyer."

"Who is it?"

"Your wife." Sam bit his lower lip. "I have to take you down in ten minutes. If you want."

"I'll be ready."

He was a convicted killer, a man others would always view as capable of killing again. So now, every time he was in a room with another person, he would be shackled—hands and feet. When Jenny walked into the meeting room, backlighting made her look angelic, and Sam's mind flashed to her in her wedding gown walking down the aisle to him. She had been beautiful then, and even more so now.

She took the seat in front of him, her face placid, her back rigid. "Hi, Sam." Her voice was flat, with no emotion.

"Hey, Jen." He smiled.

She looked around the room but didn't make eye contact. "I wanted to see you."

He nodded, but didn't speak.

"I have to say something." She shook her head, trying to find the right words. "I'm so. . . ." She couldn't form the sentence.

Sam stared at her. "I'm really glad you came. I'm having a rough time, and seeing your face helps a little."

With a huff, she pushed her chair back and began pacing the room. For the next thirty seconds, she walked in circles, muttering to herself, arms gesticulating. Near the far side of the room, she took a deep breath and returned to her seat. She closed her eyes and, when they opened, stared straight at Sam.

"I don't care anymore if you're having a rough time, and I have no interest in helping you."

Sam blinked, bewildered.

"Don't give me that 'How can you say that to me?' look." She slapped both hands in her lap. "You have humiliated me. You've lied and lied to me. I'm not going to be the prim, supportive wife anymore."

He worked hard to formulate a response. "I haven't lied to you. I need you."

"That's crap, and I don't care. I read every text you sent that woman. They flashed them up on the screen. It was disgusting. She's a tramp, and you were chasing her. We were married." Jenny's words flew out of her mouth faster than she could control.

His eyes widened. "You kicked me out of the house. What did you want me to do?"

"I told you I needed some space. I wasn't sure then, but I'm sure now. You chased after that woman. You drove up for a secret meeting and had dinner with her. What else did you do?"

"Nothing."

"I can't believe a word that comes out of your mouth. Did you sleep with her?"

"No."

"Did you want to? Did you try?"

Sam's mouth moved, but nothing came out. He closed his lips.

Jenny nodded. "That's what I thought." She paused to make sure he understood. "Maybe I could overlook your juvenile crush on that woman, but oh my god, what did you do?"

"I didn't do anything."

"You didn't do anything? You killed that man. I can't believe it, but you killed him." She stopped and then asked, "Why?"

"I didn't do it. You've got to believe me."

"I don't, and I never will. I heard all the evidence. You were there and shot the poor man in the head. I saw the pictures."

"Jen, you have to believe me."

She shook her head. "I can't and I won't. Now, you listen to me. I'm so mad, and hurt, and shocked, but I'm learning to get over it. I sat through the whole trial and never said a word. I was the dutiful wife, sitting in the back of that courtroom with my hands crossed. No more. I can't stand to look at you after what you did. I can't believe we were ever married."

Sam tried to interrupt. "Jen, I need you. Please."

She stopped looking at him but kept talking. "I'm done. We're done. I needed to say this to your face. This is the last time you will ever see me. I won't write you. I won't come to visit you, and I won't ever say your name again. And don't think about contacting Nate. I haven't said your name to him since you were arrested. I didn't think he'd understand. He's young, and he's going to forget everything about you. I'm not going to help him remember. Not a trace of you is left in the house and hopefully, soon enough, I won't have any memory of you either."

She stood, staring at him.

"I didn't do it, Jen," he said in a hoarse voice, his shoulders sagging.

"I don't believe anything you say." She pulled her wedding ring off her finger and flung it at him. It bounced off the glass partition and rolled away.

She shot him a smug glance before turning on her heels and walking out of the room.

Chapter 60

THE COURTROOM WAS SILENT, nearly empty, devoid of the tense atmosphere typical of a trial, for the outcome was no longer in doubt. Light filtered through the high windows, casting a faint glow on the long wooden benches.

After a moment of hesitation, Sam shuffled in through the side door, flanked by hulking deputies. His shackles clanked with every step. He was clean-shaven, including his head, and appeared weary and worn. Judge Denby glared down from the bench, waiting for him to take his seat.

Sam caught a glimpse of his mother sitting alone in the second row, her expression somber. She wore a dark gray pantsuit, with a flowered silk scarf draped around her neck. Like her son, she appeared shrunken and diminished. The sight of her altered appearance staggered Sam, and he wished she had stayed away to avoid witnessing his demise.

Compared to the emotional turmoil of the trial, this moment felt almost anticlimactic. Gina wasn't there—Marcia McBride had instructed her to stay away. With the prosecutor's help, Gina had prepared a searing affidavit describing in vivid detail the impact of

Pablo's murder on her life. "I hold no sympathy for the man who entered my bedroom and, with chilling precision, murdered my husband. He has shown no remorse, and his conduct during the trial has only deepened the pain his actions have caused. I believe only a sentence of life imprisonment without the chance of parole would offer me any peace."

In front of Sam's mother, cast in shadow, Gregg stood, his black suit immaculate, and turned toward Sam, offering a faint smile. This small gesture only fueled Sam's anger toward Gregg, interpreting it as smugness. The bastard can harass women with no consequences, but I do nothing and am about to be sentenced to prison, he thought.

As he sat next to Gregg, memories of their shared history flooded his mind—high school, college, camp, law school, every basketball game they played, every pitcher of beer they shared. The weight of their years together felt too heavy. He reached forward and offered his hand to Gregg, who quickly reciprocated.

McBride sat at her counsel table, offering no glances toward anyone. Today wasn't the day for grand speeches or even playful exchanges with Gregg. She would allow the judge the space to impose Sam's sentence, and hopefully, not have to utter a word. Afterward, she would watch Sam be dragged from the courtroom and begin preparations for her Senate campaign.

Denby adjusted his glasses and cleared his throat, demanding the courtroom's attention. "Mr. Jordan," he began, his voice measured, "you have been found guilty by a jury of your peers of first-degree murder." Each word fell like a heavy weight in the silence, the gravity of the moment suffocating the air.

Sam forced himself to look at the judge, his jaw trembling slightly.

Denby continued, "This court is charged with determining a sentence that reflects the severity of your crime, a crime that has impacted not only the victim's family but also the community as a whole."

Sam's gaze drifted to his mother, her head bowed in grief. Gregg's presence beside him provided a sliver of strength to face the judge's next words.

"I have considered the arguments presented by both sides," the judge said. "The defense has highlighted your previous clean record, your youth, and the testimonials from friends and colleagues. The prosecution, however, has emphasized the calculated nature of your actions, the planning and premeditation that led you here."

"Therefore, I sentence you, Samuel Jordan," Judge Denby declared, his voice resonating, "to a prison term of no less than twenty-five years and no more than forty years. You shall be transferred to the custody of the Pennsylvania Department of Corrections and serve your sentence at SCI Rockview, a maximum-security facility." The judge's ruling ensured Sam would be locked up in one of the state's most secure prisons, home to some of its most dangerous criminals.

The judge slammed his gavel.

Sam's entire body slumped. Though the sentence hadn't surprised him, it still took the breath out of him. Gregg leaned in
and whispered, "This isn't over, Sam. We have an appeals process.
Don't give up."

But despite Gregg's entreaty, Sam had long ago given up hope.
He had resigned himself to a life behind bars. The two guards
approached, and he stood to be led out of the courtroom. His
mother rushed to him, wrapping her arms around him, kissing his
cheek before he was forced to leave. As he was escorted away, the
clanging of his shackles echoed against the cold tile floor.

He didn't look back as they guided him through the door.

Chapter 61

ONCE AGAIN, SAM SAT in the meeting room at the jail, shackled and unable to stand, waiting for his next visitor. It was transfer day—he was being moved to the high-security prison in Bellefonte—but before the guards came to retrieve him, they informed him that one last person insisted on seeing him before he left.

Sam knew who it was, yet he still didn't know what to expect. His emotions swung wildly, from acceptance of his fate to near uncontrolled rage at his circumstances. He couldn't decide which version of himself would appear for this encounter.

As he waited, he struggled to gain control of the simmering anger always lurking just beneath the surface. When the door finally opened, a sardonic smile spread across his face. He leaned forward, taking in the scene.

She walked in like a celebrity entering a crowded restaurant—wanting to be seen but not approached. Dressed in all black, with a sleek, silk button-down top clinging to her curves, and hanging just above the waist of her equally form-fitting pants. Her low-riding, pointed-heeled boots clicked against the floor as she moved toward him. Her jet-black hair was pulled back, emphasizing her dark eyes, which were framed by a solid line of mascara. A small purse, its leather strap slung over her shoulder, completed the ensemble.

The smirk on her lips was exactly as he remembered it. "Hello, Sam," she said, sitting across from him. Her voice was calm, her eyes drilling into his.

Almost under his breath, he replied, "Hello, Gina."

She nodded to the guard, who turned and exited through the back door. They were alone.

"I made special arrangements to see you," she said, smooth as silk. "The prosecutor has a lot of influence around here. I wanted privacy." She spread her arms. "And now we have it. I can speak without worry." She leaned back in her chair. "They assured me I'd be safe."

Sam held out his arms exposing his cuffs and chains. "Even if I were prone to violence, there's not much I could do."

She smiled, unfazed. "You're not a violent man." She let the comment hang in the air, sitting back with a smug look.

"Why are you here?" he asked, his voice flat.

"I wanted to make sure you knew I have no hard feelings," she said. "I only have positive regard for you."

Sam's stomach churned, but he didn't respond.

She reached into her pocket and pulled out a piece of gum, carefully unwrapping it before popping it into her mouth.

"I wanted a final conversation before you left for your new home," she continued, her smile both sincere and devious. "So the record is clear, I know you didn't kill Pablo. And I know you already knew that."

He shook his head, anger and resignation warring within him. "Tell me what happened," he demanded.

"Patience, my friend," she replied with a casual smile. "Let's start at the beginning." She looked up at the ceiling as if recalling a distant memory. "Pablo was a good man—a better provider. When we first met, we had a lot of fun. I knew he would take care of me. He was very committed to me." She paused, ensuring Sam was paying attention. "Turns out he was a really smart businessman. Really smart. I didn't have much, always spent more than I made, and Pablo thought it was a good idea to have me sign a prenup. I was young and stupid. I signed it. Now, I'd never do that. But I did."

She pulled the gum from her mouth, wrapped it in the paper, and placed it on the table. Sam stared at the wad for a moment but then refocused on Gina.

"And then his business took off. He was making a boatload of money, which I liked. He started spending more time at work, away on business. But I realized I actually enjoyed it when he was gone. I started hanging out with other men, if you know what I mean. Might have even made a couple of trips to California to spend time with a mutual friend."

Sam's gaze fixed on her. None of this surprised him, but the absolute audacity of her rubbing his face in it stung. The thought of her with other men made the anger inside him flare. He spat out, "Why are you telling me this?"

"Because I like you, and I thought you deserved to know."

"You're nuts."

She laughed. "Let me finish before you judge me. So, like I said, I started getting bored with Pablo. He put on a few pounds. Yuck. He should've had more respect for me. You saw the pictures of him; he wasn't taking care of himself."

Sam thought, you mean the pictures of him with his head half blown off? "I didn't notice if he had put on any weight," he muttered.

"Well, he did. Anyway, I was stuck. I couldn't divorce him because I wouldn't get anything, but staying together was becoming tedious. So, I started thinking of a different solution. And one day, I'm on social media and there you pop up. Nice boy, Sam Jordan. I remembered you from long ago. And it turns out you didn't live far from me. I thought about what to say before I made contact."

"You mean you planned it all out. Nothing was real?"

"Pretty much. Look at the texts they put up at trial. They were friendly, nothing suggestive. I made them seem like I had a great marriage, and maybe you and I could become friends. I realized someday, strangers might read them."

Sam recalled how their reconnection had played out. She was right—the texts had been harmless. It was the phone calls that had gotten him excited, believing he had a chance with her.

"I loved our talks on the phone," she said with a seductive lilt. "They were so sexy. I heard your breathing. And no one else would ever know what I said to you. I knew I'd get you to come up and meet me for dinner. You did it so willingly, so eagerly."

"You never wanted anything else. It was all a game."

"It wasn't a game, Sam. It was important. Deadly important." She chuckled. "You remember our dinner? You were so charming. All I had to do was tilt my head and smile. You were smitten, weren't you?" He didn't respond. "Anyway, I wanted to leave with a little piece of you. I needed something, and I got it. I'm quite proud of that."

Sam furrowed his brow, confused. She reached into her small purse and pulled out a white cloth, folding it into a rectangle. "Do you recognize this?" she asked, holding it out.

Sam stared at it for a moment. "No," he said slowly.

"This is a napkin from Oakley's," she said, her voice lowering. "I used it to wipe the blood from your hand. Remember? We had our toast, and I was so clumsy—smashed my wine glass into yours. Your glass shattered, and you were bleeding all over your hand. I wiped it with this napkin. I think I even kissed your wrist before you went to wash off."

Her eyebrows arched. "There was so much blood. When you went to clean it, I tucked the napkin into my purse. Saved it for later."

It hit Sam like a ton of bricks. "My DNA. You had my DNA."

She nodded. "I kept it for a bit. Remember how we almost kissed in the parking lot? You'd have been a really good kisser. Too bad you won't be able to use those skills for a while. I texted you saying I never wanted to see you again, but then called and suggested dinner, a hotel room. . . . Sorry, I must've been sending such mixed messages."

Now everything made sense. He understood how it had all gone so wrong.

"Everything I wanted the prosecution to use was in our texts. Everything to get you to come see me was said on the phone. When I testified at the trial, I could say anything about those conversations, and no one would question it. I might have told you I was dying to see you, but I told the jury you were harassing me, making me nervous. And they believed me."

"It was all pre-planned."

"Sam, you were so sweet. You followed the script perfect-ly—buying a drink at the restaurant, checking into the ho-tel, trashing the room. The prosecutor said you might be the biggest idiot ever, using your credit card all over the neighbor-hood. You were so helpful." She laughed, and then got serious. "But I never thought you were an idiot."

He stared at her, speechless.

"Before you got to the restaurant," she continued, "I said my goodbyes to Pablo. Well, first I made him have sex with me. Going out with a bang, I guess." She chuckled to herself. "Getting the gun wasn't hard. I didn't use my credit card to buy it. I got some of your blood off that napkin and mixed it with the blood on the walls. I scraped some under Pablo's fingernails, then left the house. I should've smashed a window, made it look like you broke in, but I forgot. I was under pressure to run to the mall, get back, and report my husband's murder. I dumped the gun on the way. Made a couple of purchases making sure I used my credit card. Came home and walked in on that horrific crime scene. Called 911. You have to admit, I sounded pretty scared, didn't I?"

Sam nodded, expressionless.

"They never considered me as a suspect. I pointed to our texts, and they ate it up. Once the DNA came back, you were toast."

Sam had suspected something all along. He and Gregg had mused about Gina being the only other person with a reason to kill Pablo, but they had no evidence to point at her. Nothing they could use in court. Without anything incriminating, suggesting she murdered her husband would not have gone over well with the jury. Ignoring her as a suspect hadn't worked either.

"So, nothing with you was real."

"Oh, Sam. Everything about this is real. Look at you—you're in jail. I do feel bad about that."

He scoffed. "I'm sure you feel really bad about it."

She hesitated. "I do. But I'm in the place I wanted to be. I'm going to sell Pablo's business. For a lot. I don't have much to worry about. I wanted to say I'm sorry. You're such a nice guy. But I guess that's your problem—too trusting. Little suggestion," she reached toward him, causing him to jerk back. "Don't be so trusting in your next place. It could get you into trouble."

Gina rose from her chair and glanced at her watch. "I need to go. It was great seeing you again. Thanks for everything you've done for me. We won't be talking for a while, so take care."

She gave a small wave to signal the guard. Sam watched her sashay out of the room, her exit like smoke drifting into the ether. Another wave of anger surged through him, but he quelled it with acceptance that he had no reason to suspect that his unyielding trust in her was misplaced.

Chapter 62

THE TRANSFER TO THE Rockview State Penitentiary occurred without issue. Sam, like all the inmates there, was placed in a high-security cell with one other person, Dan—a large black man who demonstrated little inclination to engage in conversation. This suited Sam just fine, as it allowed him the space to think, and the time—which he would have in abundance—to read.

Often, his mind wandered back to the carefree days at camp when his biggest worry was whether Gina liked him. He recognized now how juvenile he had been back then, but wasn't that the prerogative of being young?

He didn't dwell on the trial as much anymore, understanding what she had done. If he let his mind focus too much on the injustice of his situation, his anger would consume him. Instead, he worked to accept his fate and gain some insight.

At times, thoughts of the present and past would merge, and he could see the evolution of the people and their relationships with him. Gregg had been his friend since his teens, and he realized he wasn't responsible for his current plight. They exchanged letters, and Gregg wrote that he wanted to visit. Hopefully soon.

Sam's mind drifted and somehow landed on Trevor Morrison. How had that dude ended up testifying at trial? What had Gina said to him? Trevor had testified that Sam told him he wanted to get with Gina. Sam pondered his testimony. He didn't remember any conversation with Trevor. He had always been too cool for Sam, and they never hung out. Besides, it was Trevor who was with Gina, not Sam.

Sam rested his head on his pillow, and in the hazy fog of near sleep, his mind drifted back to the past.

Like most days at camp, the weather bordered on idyllic. A few clouds drifted across the sky, and the sun warmed the lakefront. Sam had his shirt off, and his long swim trunks covered most of his legs. The late summer sun sat high in the sky, and his skin had bronzed.

He stared out over the lake and watched the seven sunfish sailboats dart across the water. The kids were skilled enough to sail the boats without a counselor aboard, and their loud voices carried back to shore. Gregg and another counselor were in one of the boats, making sure the kids stayed safe, so Sam didn't have much to do. He took a seat on a milk crate and tilted his head up toward the sun. Its rays warmed his face.

As he rested, aware of the boats skirting around the lake but not really paying attention, he heard someone drag another milk crate next to him.

"Mind if I hang with you?" Trevor Morrison said, shirtless and sporting Ray-Bans on top of his head.

Sam nodded. "My milk crate is your milk crate."

Trevor laughed, probably a bit too hard, and slapped Sam on the back. "Most considerate of you."

They sat without saying a word for a few minutes, the kids' yells and laughter from the lake washing over them.

Trevor interrupted the quiet to engage in some small talk, something about being late to the beach and his kids already being on the sailboats, so he was getting to take advantage of the downtime. Sam listened and grunted in agreement, but it wasn't much of a conversation.

Then the subject matter shifted. Trevor straightened up and turned toward Sam. "Hey, you're friends with Gina, right?" Trevor asked.

"Sure, so are you."

Trevor hesitated. "Yeah, I am. What do you think of her?"

Sam sensed shaky terrain. "She's great. You know that."

"Sure. You ever think something's off with her?"

Sam shook his head.

"It's just, sometimes I think something's odd with her. She can be so friendly and energized, and then she turns quiet and dark."

"I haven't seen it. Don't know what to say."

"I mean, she can be so passionate." This was the last thing Sam wanted to hear. "She's hot, you know? Like, would you want to go out with her, just looking at her from afar?"

"Sure, I'd like to get with her," Sam said, not wanting any part of this discussion. "She's awesome; anyone would, but you're the one who's with her, not me."

"See, you get it. She can be so much fun, but when we're alone, she turns quiet and distant. But she comes back real quick, like nothing ever happened. I don't know, there's something dark inside of her, I think. Sometimes when we're fooling around, it's like she's not all there. Like her mind is somewhere else, plotting something evil. Once we were making out, and I opened my eyes, and she was just staring at me. She was kissing me, but her mind was focused on something else. So weird. What do you think?"

"Well," Sam struggled to add to the conversation, "I guess you enjoy the good times. It's a summer fling."

"Yeah, you're right. Most of the time, we have lots of fun. We're all leaving for the summer in a week. We probably won't see each other again after we leave." He elbowed Sam. "After the summer's over, she's all yours."

The kids were bringing in the sailboats, so Sam didn't get a chance to respond, which was fortuitous because he had nothing to say.

Sam stared at the fluorescent light above his bed. Once again, Gina dominated his thoughts. Despite her reappearance in his life, he hadn't remembered the conversation with Trevor at the lake, but boom—there it was, popping into his head like it was yesterday. Damn, Trevor's testimony at trial was essentially right. He had told him he wanted to get with Gina. It was completely out of context and ignored the premonition Trevor had about the evil in Gina's soul. Was Trevor giving him some kind of warning back then? Who knew? But Sam had never paid it any mind and had tucked the conversation away in the recesses of his memory, so in his thoughts she still remained the same cutie he pined for at camp.

Now, he had a much more sanguine view of her. He would never talk to Trevor Morrison again, but if he did, he would listen much more closely to what he had to say.

He let out a heavy sigh, causing Big Dan to rumble in his nap, and allowed his thoughts to drift until he pictured Gina walking along the beach at camp, her hair blowing in the wind.

I wonder what she's doing now, he thought.

James Rosenberg has been a practicing attorney for nearly thirty-five years. He spends much of his time in a courtroom and has cross-examined every type of witness imaginable.

Every trial is a story and the people involved believe that their case is the most important in the world. When you listen to these people, they have great stories to tell.

When not trying cases, James spends much time with his wife and three kids. They are getting older now, but also have great stories to tell.

Sometimes, when everyone is out of the house, James gets to talk to Allie the wonder dog. She is a great listener.

T HE VERDICTS AND VINDICATION SERIES

If you enjoyed this selection from the Verdicts and Vindication series, please check out the other books in the series:

Each book in the Verdicts and Vindication series provides an enhanced look into what a lawyer endures in taking a case to trial. From the beginning of the case, to the jury's verdict, you will experience the sacrifice, intelligence, and often, the courage it takes to push a case to the end. Every case takes a toll on the litigants and the lawyers, and the ramifications of even the simplest trials extend far beyond the courtroom and into the lives of the people who participate in a trial.

D EAR READERS,

Thank you so much for taking the time and energy to read *Fatal Reunion*. To me, knowing that people out there are reading my books makes the long hours of writing and editing even more worthwhile. While I mainly write for personal reasons, I get so much personal satisfaction when readers let me know they enjoyed what they have read.

One way you can help me is to review the books you have read. Reviews help prospective readers determine if a book they are considering is one they want to try. With Amazon's algorithms, reviews also help a book get more attention.

Please consider leaving a review on Amazon.

Reviews on Goodreads and Bookbub are also helpful.

You can also check out my website at jamesrosenberglegalthrillers.com

Made in United States
Troutdale, OR
06/24/2025

32354159R00176